Dear Alex,

Lovely to meet a
fellow from Cheltenham.
I look forward to
learning from you — I
love your sense of
balance & fun.

Roger Dean

Praise for Be. Do. Live.

PERSONAL AND PROFESSIONAL DEVELOPMENT EXPERTS

"*Be. Do. Live.* is a terrific book that can change lives. Rajeev Dewan has taken knowledge and learnings from throughout the world and synthesized them into readable, bite-sized nuggets of wisdom. The result is a practical guidebook that is at once insightful and actionable."

—STEPHEN M. R. COVEY
author of *The New York Times* bestseller, *The Speed of Trust*

"Rajeev Dewan's new book offers us a useful, engaging method for getting clear about what really matters in all aspects of our lives and taking practical action to pursue our most precious goals with vigor. A powerful, significant achievement!"

—DR. STEWART D. FRIEDMAN
best-selling author of *Total Leadership: Be a Better Leader,
Have a Richer Life*, and Founding Director of both the
Wharton Leadership Program and the Wharton Work/
Life Integration Project, University of Pennsylvania

"This is a wonderfully insightful book that helps you ask the questions and make the decisions that assure you live a happy, successful and prosperous life."

—BRIAN TRACY
author of *The Way to Wealth*

"*Be. Do. Live.* is an integrated blueprint to an exceptional life! It closes the gap between who you are, what you do, and, ultimately, how you live."

—MARSHALL GOLDSMITH
author of *The New York Times* bestseller
What Got You Here Won't Get You There,
the 2007 Harold Longman Award-winning
business book of the year

"Rajeev has an amazing ability to synthesize wisdom. This book is the category killer . . . it's the singular work on personal development and life leadership."

—MATT CHURCH
Creator of Thought Leaders and best-selling author

"In *Be. Do. Live.* Rajeev Dewan offers all of us a precious gift, the gift of an effective, easy-to-use, empowering approach to living the life that is our destiny. He teaches us how to unleash the potential within us while addressing the blockages that often hold us back. Moreover, he's written a book that's truly enjoyable to read with the concepts presented in a visually dynamic manner. This book is relevant for all generations and all cultures. Thank you, Rajeev!"

—RAY JEFFERSON
Leadership Facilitator & Speaker,
McKinsey leadership consultant ('06-'08) &
White House Fellow ('00-'01); MBA, Harvard Business School

CEOs

"*Be. Do. Live.* is a work of great generosity and spirit. Rajeev Dewan's uplifting desire to live a full life and help others do the same is evident on every page."

—KEITH FERRAZZI
CEO, Ferrazzi Greenlight, and
The New York Times best-selling author of *Never Eat Alone*

"*Be. Do. Live.* is a practical book that tells us the few things that make all the difference in creating and sustaining an outstanding quality of life. A remarkable book, it quickly gets to the core of what really matters in designing and living a life of purpose, passion and peace."

—SARTHAK BEHURIA
Chairman, Indian Oil Corporation Ltd.

"This book refreshingly addresses the **total** person. It provides many challenging ideas and observations concerning the strength and frailty of the human species. A fascinating read and a great reference source with very practical solutions and suggestions about living your life!"

—PETER SCOTT
Chairman, Sinclair Knight Merz

"*Be. Do. Live.* is a special book that will enrich the lives of those who read it. In the 21st century, life is extremely busy and it's important that we take the time to answer the insightful questions in Rajeev's book. Whether you are a parent, a friend, a colleague or a business leader, take the time to read this book to discover your purpose and passion, and improve all aspects of your life."

—STEVE TUCKER
CEO, MLC

"Rajeev's book offers insightful perspectives for living an authentic and harmonious life. *Be. Do. Live.* provides a holistic blueprint to help ambitious professionals resolve the sometimes inherent conflicts that exist between their personal and professional aspirations. A powerful blend of head, heart and spirit—once I started reading it, I couldn't put it down!"

—ROB CHANDRA
Managing Partner, Bessemer Venture Partners;
MBA, Harvard Business School

"Mark Twain wrote, *'Make no small plans. They have no magic to move men's minds.'* In *Be. Do. Live.* Rajeev shows us how to plan the most important thing of all—a life, our own life. By pulling together so many ideas, concepts, thoughts and techniques about life, and assembling them in an easy and meaningful flow, Rajeev also shows us how to create the magic needed to move minds. Once I started reading it and 'doing it', I had to finish it. It reminded me of the magic in my own life. Thank you Rajeev."

—MICHAEL MORGAN
CEO, Herrmann International Asia, The Whole Brain Company

"*Be. Do. Live.* is a must-have, a must-read and a must-apply book for people in all walks of life, anywhere in the world. It makes you think deeply about what is most important to you, and how to *Be. Do. Live.* in a way that maximizes your success and happiness, not just in the moment, but also over your entire lifetime. *Be. Do. Live.* would have to rank as one of the most inspiring, empowering and immediately useful book I have ever read."

—S.K. JAIN
Director LPG, Bharat Petroleum Corporation Ltd;
former Executive Chairman, Petroleum India International

"In *Be. Do. Live.* Rajeev Dewan provides an inspirational road map for your personal and professional success. Full of wisdom, insights and actionable strategies, *Be. Do. Live.* is an excellent resource for individuals committed to creating and sustaining an all-round rich quality of life. I am convinced that *Be. Do. Live.* will change the way you think and the way you act. I urge you to read this wonderful book. It will absolutely help you to change your life for the better!"

—KANWAL WADHAWAN
Chairman and CEO of Global Telelinks, Inc.

"Rajeev Dewan's *Be. Do. Live.* is a great find for business leaders and their people. In his book, Dewan zeroes in on the ultimate challenge of the new millennium—how to create and sustain a successful and fulfilling life. *Be. Do. Live.* achieves this goal by providing a robust road map, both for individuals and organizations. The true genius of the book is its universal relevance, as it combines timeless wisdom with a highly effective common-sense approach to enhancing your professional and personal life. A must read!"

—MICHAEL WILKINSON
CEO, Leadership Strategies;
author of *The Secrets of Facilitation*

"No matter where you are in your career or in your relationships or in a way of living your life, Rajeev Dewan's book will be of immense help to you. Dewan has taken the best of psychology and philosophy, both from the East and the West, and very insightfully packaged it into practical ready-to-apply wisdom. No matter who you are or what your background is, every page in this book is powerful enough to transform your life."

—KAMAL SARMA

Managing Director, Rezilium;
Founder, Institute of Mental Resilience;
author of *Mental Resilience: The Power of Clarity*

"A book for our time. Using a blend of eastern and western philosophy, Dewan is masterful in showing us the path to realizing a balance of achievement and contribution in our lives. Insightful and highly practical it is a must read for those seeking to maximize their effectiveness in order to make a difference."

—SUREN JAYATILLEKE

CEO, The Axcess Solutions Group

GLOBAL CONSULTING EXECUTIVES

"Dewan offers a fresh and vital take on the *'change your life for good'* genre of business-oriented personal development books. And wow! it genuinely works. *Be. Do. Live.* is packed with pragmatic, action-oriented levers and jaw-droppingly insightful exercises—all based on a synthesis of some of the most powerful ideas in personal development coupled with timeless philosophical thought. The ideas in this book will change the rest of your life!"

—RICHARD G. BHANAP

Managing Director, KPMG LLP

"I live by the adage *'if you only do what you have only done, then you will only get what you've always gotten'*—in *Be. Do. Live.* Rajeev has provided the one-stop-shop to help anyone who is willing to try to be who they really are and to live a better life for themselves and others. Full of personal stories, simply but elegantly constructed, it brings all the wisdom of the ages and self help theories to life. I am an avid reader of books of this nature—it is a joy and relief to find so much of the wisdom of ten's of thousand's of pages in one place. I have been on a journey."

—SANDRA BIRKENSLEIGH
Senior Partner, PricewaterhouseCoopers

"*Be. Do. Live.* is filled with practical wisdom for people who want to take control of their lives—relationships, careers and personal development. Each time I read a chapter, I get valuable new insights. I've seen Rajeev consistently demonstrate these practices for the past decade. This book has the gift of being simple without being simplistic."

—GINO DIGREGORIO
Partner, Accenture

"Rajeev has brought together his boundless energy, passion for lifelong learning, and practical experience in this wonderful collection of insights and tools. A fantastic resource to dip into time and again to help us all be the person we want to be and live the life we want to live!"

—CHLOE HAWCROFT
Director, People and Change, Advisory,
PricewaterhouseCoopers

"*Be. Do. Live.* is a critical read for all leaders in our world—whether you lead a nation, a company, a team, your family, or even yourself—you will find this book to be a fantastic resource. *Be. Do. Live.* is readable, practical, and broadly applicable. The equivalent of an entire library of success literature is found in this book. Read this book and pass it to everyone that you care about."

—SAMEERA QAZI
Management Consultant, MBA, Harvard Business School

"As a corporate professional there are many journeys to choose from and numerous paths we must take. It is easy to get lost in the myriad of travels we find ourselves taking each day. *Be. Do. Live.* is the wakeup call that every professional—unconsciously or consciously, caught up in the all-consuming commercial world—needs. *Be. Do. Live.* is the alarm bell which will empower you to stop, take a moment and consider, whether what you are doing in your day to day life is really providing you with the satisfaction, pleasure, sense of well-being and freedom you desire. *Be. Do. Live.* is an insightful, thought provoking and inspiring read. It will encourage the pursuit of happiness and excellence in all aspects of your life."

—JULIE CHANDRA
Senior Associate, Corrs Chambers Westgarth

"When I received this book and was asked by Rajeev Dewan to read it and offer my comments, my first instinct was, *'I don't have the time and I'm not a big fan of so called self-help books.'* However, as I read the introduction, and then the first few chapters, I was delighted at the depth of the book and the insights I derived, literally from every page. It made me think and reflect deeply about my own life, at so many different levels. This book gets to the core roots of what creates a great life. Dewan discusses with clarity and insight: how to know yourself, be yourself, evolve yourself and make a meaningful contribution to society. Everyone should take the time to read this book."

—TONY SIMKINS
Senior Executive, Management Consultant, LLM (1st Class),
B.Bus Computing (Distinction), MBA

GENERAL MANAGERS

"For many people everyday life is a struggle. For many others each day is a new joy. What's the difference? It's the ability of a person to confront a challenge, learn, overcome and a hit a new level. *Be. Do. Live.* is a book that gives you simple yet profound ways to learn and grow."

—GREG MILLER
General Manager, MLC Advice Solutions

"In *Be. Do. Live.* Rajeev Dewan offers us a sustainable model for holistic leadership that is based on timeless principles and innovative strategies. This book provides a refreshingly unique proposition for individuals who strive to be their very best—both personally and professionally. An invaluable addition to every leader's library."

—JOSHUA FARRELL
General Manager, FranklinCovey,
Australia and New Zealand

"Powerful on many levels, *Be. Do. Live.* provides an efficient and articulate blueprint for deep reflection and self-awareness. It is a powerful synthesis of the very best of East & West, and old & new ideas into an action plan for immediate and permanent change for the better."

—ANOOP PRAKASH
former McKinsey consultant, and Vice President, LexisNexis;
MBA, Harvard Business School

"An absolute must-read for aspiring professionals and entrepreneurs who want to significantly increase their effectiveness in the workplace and at home. Dewan has created a brilliant blueprint for both career and personal success in today's challenging times."

—MARK RANTALL
Managing Director, Godfrey Pembroke

"*Be. Do. Live.* will inspire and empower you to lead a more fulfilling life. This book is a must-read for everyone who is looking to attain new heights in his or her life."

—DAVID "BULL" GURFEIN
Vice President of Casino Marketing, The Venetian/The Palazzo;
Lieutenant Colonel (retd), US Marine Corps

"Linking east to west thinking, Rajeev reminds us of the power of the individual to achieve their own greatness if they dare and provides pathways to that personal greatness. *Be. Do. Live.* provides a mind-set, a skill-set, and a tool-set for anyone wanting to fully ignite their own potential, whilst helping others to do the same."

—TONY SATTOUT
General Manager, MLC; Dean, The Academy

"Dewan does an excellent job of turning universal wisdom into simple, practical tools that readers can apply in their everyday lives. In this book, you will find rich insights into how to make a life—not just a living. *Be. Do. Live.* is a perfect blend of wisdom, inspiration and practical experience and a definite must-read!"

—STEPHEN DURKIN
State General Manager (NSW & ACT),
National Australia Bank

"*Be. Do. Live.* is a book for everyone who wish to deepen their self-awareness and aspire to personal achievement and greatness. It is a passionate call to action, challenging you to remember who you really are and to let your light shine."

—MARK HUA
Account Director, Ericsson, U.K.

"This book is a brilliantly written, masterful distillation of *'successful'* philosophies and practices . . . some simple, some profound, and all *'essential'* in today's complex world. A must-read, and a must-apply!"

—TONY EID
Chief Operating Officer (Applications),
Challenger Financial Services Group

"There is nothing more important you can do than create a life that matters for you and your family. In *Be. Do. Live.* Dewan shows the readers how to achieve enduring success in all aspects of life, while staying true to who they are. This book is a valuable practical resource for all leaders and everyone else wanting to take their life to the next level of success and beyond."

—REBECCA NASH
General Manager, People and Organizational Development,
National Australia Bank

"A great compendium of wisdom to help guide you through the twists and turns of life."

—ALEX TICHON
Head of Program Office, BT Financial Group

EXECUTIVE AND SPORTS COACHES

"Exceptionally Compelling . . . Rajeev Dewan provides profound insights and offers you practical tools to help you close the gap between where you are and where you want to be. Applying the wisdom in this book will result in an even more authentic, vibrant and all-round fulfilled life. A must-read!"

—JOHN DRURY
Executive Coach, former Fortune 100 Chief Marketing Officer,
author of *Awaken Your Soul*

"Whether you are leading a team, an organization or your family, *Be. Do. Live.* is a terrific resource and will be of immense help. No matter who you are or what your background is, I am sure reading this book will change your life. It gives practical experiences from both east and west all of which can be applied in our everyday lives."

—LALCHAND RAJPUT
Coach of the Winning Indian Cricket Team,
Twenty20 World Cup, 2007

"*Be. Do. Live.* deftly combines reflection practices and action nuggets in a high-octane roadmap for aware, vibrant living. The take-home value is immediate and plentiful."

—JIM WARNER
author of *Aspirations of Greatness*

"*Be. Do. Live.* gives you the blueprint for a successful life. It's an honest, straightforward and telling experience of how to succeed and how to be fulfilled."

—MARGARET STUART
Founder, MangoTiger Career & Life Transitions,
author of *Switch on your Brain*

RESEARCH AND ACADEMIC AUTHORITIES

"*Be. Do. Live.* is much more than a book. It is a vehicle that will transform your life if you mull over the concepts it lays out and internalize them. The excellent news is that it will improve your work life and effectiveness every bit as much as it will improve your personal life."

—DR. SRIKUMAR S. RAO
Adjunct Professor, London Business School &
Haas School of Business at University of California, Berkeley;
author of *Are YOU Ready to Succeed: Unconventional Strategies for Achieving Personal Mastery in Business and Life*

"For anyone who has grappled with difficult choices in their personal and professional lives, this book offers a powerful and pragmatic set of tools and insights to navigate those decisions effectively."

—SAILESH CHUTANI
Ph.D., former Senior Director & Founder,
External Research and Programs Group, Microsoft Research

"As a consultant, university lecturer and mother, it's not easy for me to find time to read self-improvement books. Rajeev's book is packed full of bite-sized wisdom and food-for-thought that is easily accessible when you need that extra "lift". It's like a vitamin supplement for authentic, abundant living."

—STEPHANIE OWEN
B.Ec., MBA, Management Consultant,
Adjunct Faculty Member, Macquarie Graduate School of Management

"In *Be. Do. Live.* Rajeev Dewan, has made an excellent attempt to integrate wisdom from both East and West. He has skillfully translated this rare harmonious blend into simple practical tools that one gets tempted to apply with a view to improving his/her life. There can be no two opinions that the book is both inspiring and insightful and as such a definite must-read!"

—PROFESSOR H. L. MANOCHA
Poly Institute of NYU, New York

Be. Do. Live.

Be. Do. Live.

*Ageless Wisdom Meets Modern Know-how
in a New Action Plan for Lasting Success*

RAJEEV DEWAN

Pembrook Publishing
Sydney, Australia

Published by Pembrook Publishing
PO Box 6300
North Sydney
NSW 2059, Australia

Cover Design: Dunn + Associates
Interior Design & Typesetting: Desktop Miracles, Inc.

National Library of Australia Cataloging-in-Publication Data

Author: Dewan, Rajeev.
Title: Be do live : ageless wisdom meets modern know-how in a
            new action plan for lasting success / Rajeev Dewan.
Edition: 1st ed.
ISBN: 9780980556704 (hbk.)
Subjects: 1. Self-actualization (Psychology)--Problems, exercises, etc.
            2. Leadership.
            3. Executives--Conduct of life.
            4. Quality of work life.
            5. Work and family.
Dewey Number: 158.1

Printed in Australia by McPherson's Printing Group

"Be the change you want to see in the world."

—MAHATMA GANDHI

"Knowing others is wisdom,
knowing yourself is enlightenment."

—LAO TZU
the famous Chinese philosopher

*This book is dedicated to everyone continuing to seek even
more wisdom and even more enlightenment.*

Acknowledgments

Sir Isaac Newton, often regarded as the most influential scientist in history, once said: *"If I have seen further, it is by standing on the shoulders of giants."* Likewise, this book is only alive because several giants have helped me along the way, and without their help, this book would not exist.

First and foremost, I thank my earliest teachers, my parents, Omesh Chander Dewan and Santosh Dewan. No words can express my gratitude for your unconditional love and caring. I feel blessed to have you as my parents. To my brother Tarun: Your love, guidance and encouragement have helped me to pursue my passions; you are a very special and beautiful soul.

To the numerous teachers who have helped me to become a better person, I thank you from the bottom of my heart. I especially want to express my deep gratitude to two extraordinary masters: Dr Stephen R. Covey and Anthony Robbins—your teachings have had a huge impact on my life. I also want to thank the following outstanding coaches: Eckhart Tolle, Sri Sri Ravi Shankar, Tom Peters, Marcus Buckingham, Dr Deepak Chopra, and Dr Wayne W. Dyer.

To my ultimate source of inspiration, my three beautiful girls: my wife Priya, and my daughters, Shivani and Sonali. You are the reasons why I continue to strive to be a better husband, a better father, and a better human being. To my love, Priya: I feel blessed to be with you, and I thank you for loving me, even when it's hard, which it often is! To my daughters, Shivani and Sonali: I love you deeply and thank you for being you and being two of my greatest teachers.

To my other set of parents (Kan and Reeta Kapoor): Thank you for loving me as your son and for raising the most wonderful girl, my wife. Reeta mum: You are the most loving person I know and I'm so lucky to have you in my life. Thank you also to Neerja bhabhi, Shub, Rupali, and Shabd: For your love, encouragement and support over the last two decades.

To my dearest friend, Suren Jayatilleke: If there is one person who has had the most direct influence on this book, it is you. You were the first person I shared this concept with and were it not for your continuous encouragement and unconditional help, I would have never completed this project. You are a generous soul and a great brother!

I have been fortunate to have had many mentors along my career path. A special mentor and a friend who has believed in me and backed me has been Tony Sattout. Thank you Tony for enabling my light to shine.

Thank you to the numerous people who have provided guidance and inspiration along the journey, including: Kamal Sarma, Anoop Prakash, Sameera Qazi, Tony Eid, Vic Parikh, John Tindall, Chandra Prakash, Seema Katiperi, Bill Feng, Shashi Prakash, Uncle Sah, Sanjit Roy and Melanie Collins.

A big thank you to the talented team of international experts who have supported me in bringing this book to life. This team of experts includes: Kathi Dunn and Hobie (from Dunn+Associates), Graham Van Dixhorn (from WriteToYourMarket), Robin Quinn (Brainstorm Editorial), Scott Anderson (from BusinessWritingPlus), Barry Kerrigan & Del LeMond (from Desktop Miracles) and Relmi Damiano (from Relmi Design).

Finally, I thank God for the many blessings in my life, and for using me as a vessel to spread the messages contained in this book.

Table of Contents

Introduction

Of all the words in the English language, "be," "do," and "live" are among the most common—and the most powerful. Taken together as a command, or at least as a strong suggestion, they encompass virtually all aspects of what can truly make a difference in the human condition. Who we are (being), what we accomplish (doing), and how we experience our world (living)—these are ageless and provocative issues. And while it may seem that we are inundated with "how to" advice on every topic imaginable, clearly our era is not the only one in which people have yearned to move beyond "just getting by" to a deeply fulfilling, joyful and abundant life.

From time immemorial, the great thinkers have pondered these questions and rendered their verdicts. We have a record of suggestions dating back thousands of years. Even so, anyone doubting the continued relevance of these issues to our lives today need only glance at statistics on the number of books currently available on related subjects. A recent search on Amazon.com yielded the following results:

- Philosophy   438,233
- Psychology   363,666
- Self-help   139,108
- Business   1,457,100
- Spirituality   124,677
- Relationships   453,284
- Wealth   290,772

Each of these book topics is covered in *Be. Do. Live.* But with so many books out there to help us define who we are, decide what we should do, and improve how we live, what need is there for another book? It's all been written, hasn't it? Well, no, it hasn't. As I see it, there are two major pieces that have been missed in all the talk about how to live a fuller, more satisfying life: synthesis and catalyst. Here's what I mean.

First, the sheer volume of potentially meaningful advice is essentially overwhelming to the average reader. Take me, for example. Even after reading hundreds of books on improving the quality of my life, I still felt the need to write one of my own. Granted, I had a catalyst, an experience so powerful that it compelled me to do it (more about that shortly). Still, I hadn't found what I was looking for, in part because of the magnitude of the task and the multitude of well-intentioned input. Adding to the difficulty of the endeavor, it seems that truly transformative information exists only in widely scattered pockets or clearings, often obscured by time, translation, or forests of mumbo-jumbo. So the challenge is to locate information and then sift through the useless, irrelevant, false, or downright harmful offerings to get to the stuff that's true and good.

So in large part what's been missing is a **synthesis,** a best-of-the-best compilation taken from the universe of answers to the question, *"What are the few things that make the biggest difference in creating and sustaining an outstanding quality of life?"*

Second—and this drives to the heart of *Be. Do. Live.*—who cares? Our lives are good enough, right? We're relatively comfortable, relatively successful, and relatively happy. What's the point of trying so hard to take our lives to the next level when this level, however unsatisfying and frustrating, has some redeeming qualities?

Well, this "good enough" factor is dangerous, because it can lull us into accepting a life that is painful at a deep level despite its charms. And by the time you whip up a bit of urgency about your being, doing, and living, it may be too late!

Twice in 2006, I thought I was going to die. I thought I had cancer, the scary Big C. I saw specialists and went through months of invasive tests, including X-rays, CAT scans, MRIs—the works! It was terrifying. It was hard. The anticipation of waiting for the test results was the most agonizing experience I've ever faced.

Luckily, I didn't have cancer and, barring an unforeseen accident, it's more than likely that I'll still be alive when you read these words. Another upside is that, after all of this, I feel like I've been given a second chance to live! Even though I wouldn't want to go through the mental and emotional stress and pain of those horrible months again, I'm deeply grateful for the *experience* I went through. I know it must sound weird . . . why in the world would I feel grateful for the toughest period of my life?

It's not as weird as it sounds, and here's why: The prospect of dying forced me to look, as never before, at how I was *living* my life versus how I *wanted* to live my life. That experience, that process, is at the heart of *Be. Do. Live.* So let's be clear. **This book is first and foremost about life**. It's just that the imminent prospect of my life ending "before my time" was a **catalyst,** an agent of change that fostered something immeasurably good in my life—especially since I did, in fact, live to talk about it, to write about it and, most importantly, to experience it.

Even after the risk of immediate death had receded, it became clear that I needed to make more changes, not at some point in the far-flung future, but **RIGHT NOW.** It also became crystal clear to me that somehow I was going to use my wake-up call to help other people. That's part of what makes *Be. Do. Live.* different. You, the reader, can choose to reap the benefits of my life-changing experience without the soul-shattering fear that accompanied it.

QUESTIONS BROUGHT IMPORTANT ANSWERS

What happened was that once the first immobilizing shock and fear loosened somewhat, I quickly began to feel a heightened sense of urgency to dig deeper inside myself. I started asking myself questions, deeply profound questions that I had flirted with before, but never with the same degree of intensity and urgency as I did now.

I now looked at everything through a filter reminding me that I might have only six months left. Or six weeks. Or six days! So I asked myself:

- *Am I satisfied with the person I have become?*
- *What really matters most to me?*
- *Am I living in harmony with what is most important to me?*
- *What has kept me from living in alignment with what is most important to me?*
- *What can I do now? What do I stop? What do I start? What do I change?*

Imagine that *you* only had only a short time to live. Would you live *your* life any differently from the way you are living it now? I have posed this question to men and women across the world, people with diverse backgrounds, professions, nationalities, religions, and personalities. The overwhelming response was, not surprisingly, *"Yes, I would definitely live differently if I only had a short time to live."*

In my case, a sense of urgency created by the prospect of my impending death led me to "the life of my dreams." What I learned from the experience is that creating an outstanding life is not so much about learning new concepts or acquiring new knowledge as it is about:

1. Looking at what you already know from a different perspective

AND

2. Acting on what you know more consistently

Be. Do. Live. helps you do just that. I've synthesized the best information available to help you quickly get to an even more outstanding life.

WHAT MAKES *BE. DO. LIVE.* UNIQUE?

In case you'd like a little more evidence of this book's uniqueness, I offer you the following seven factors:

1. **_Be. Do. Live._ synthesizes ageless wisdom from *both* the East and the West.** Today, as globalization takes hold, people are increasingly looking to both Eastern and Western philosophies for answers to the eternal question, *"How do I live a more authentic and satisfying life?"* Having had the privilege of living in both the East and the West, I too have sought inspiration from the wisdom of these two great civilizations, and this book is my attempt to bring together what I see as the best of Eastern and Western philosophies (ways of thinking and being) and practices (doing).

2. **The book deals with *all* the significant areas of our lives.** In *Be. Do. Live.* I focus on the **foundations** that impact both our personal and professional lives. Therefore, as you come to understand and apply the material covered here, you'll find yourself making significant progress across multiple areas of your life.

3. **It is practical and relevant to the challenges of the 21st century.** By balancing the need to make a living with the need to make a life, this book conveys messages that are both practical and easy to apply. The book doesn't just present esoteric theories; it uses common sense and shows you the fastest, most effective way to apply what you learn to your life.

4. **I have followed the 80/20 principle, focusing on the few things that make all the difference.** In a nutshell, the 80/20 principle asserts that 20% of our activities generate 80% of the results we get. This book dwells on the principles and practices in that 20% which make 80% of the difference in our lives.

5. **It cuts to the bottom line—fast.** This book is not filled with stories. There are no grand existential theories, and it's not full of reams of

facts. Instead, it focuses on the most important distinctions that have stood the test of time across centuries—the bottom line. It gets to the key messages logically, succinctly, and quickly, in a "tell-me-the-way-it-is" approach. It cuts to the chase.

6. ***Be. Do. Live.*** **is action-oriented.** Knowledge without action is useless. Every page in this book encourages you, either implicitly or explicitly, to put the material presented into action. Most chapters are self-contained and can be read in less than three minutes. As such, you can immediately start applying what you've learned, thus minimizing any delay between understanding the concept and putting the concept into action.

7. **The book combines words with visual frameworks.** As the saying goes, "A picture is worth a thousand words." Therefore, wherever it made sense, I've used visual frameworks to either articulate or reinforce concepts.

In *Be. Do. Live.* I share with you the vital few foundational philosophies and practices that will result in quantum progress across all areas of your personal and professional life. It doesn't matter what your current situation is. If you understand and apply these principles consistently, you'll experience a *quality of life more outstanding than you ever thought possible!*

WHAT MAKES A LIFE OUTSTANDING?

So what are the elements of an outstanding life? You and I will have different answers to this question, of course, but there will be some common themes, too. I suspect you'll agree that an outstanding life exhibits several of the following characteristics:

- A life based on intention and conscious design
- A life in harmony with what is most important to you

- A life in which you consistently experience love, joy, happiness, peace, and fulfillment
- A life that is abundant, prosperous, and free
- A life that maximizes your skills, talents, and potential
- A life of ongoing growth across all dimensions of body, mind, and spirit
- A life that inspires others
- A life that makes a difference in the world
- A life that you are truly proud of
- A life, no matter how long or short, which is *lived to its fullest!*

Assuming that you agree with some of these statements, how would you rate your current quality of life? I know that I personally had many gaps to fill, and while I haven't filled them all so far, my life is exponentially richer, more exciting, and more satisfying than I could ever have imagined. This, too, is my hope for you.

I also know that a book is only a tool. But I believe that books have the power to inspire us to action. Consistent action is what creates momentum, and momentum is the fundamental key to progress. So, regardless of how great or not-so-great your life is at the moment, I want this book to serve as a tool to help you move to the next level—whatever that level may be *for you.*

HOW TO GET THE MOST FROM *BE. DO. LIVE.*

Archimedes, the Greek inventor and mathematician, once said this famous line: *"Give me a lever long enough and a fulcrum on which to place it, and I shall move the world."* The concept of leverage isn't difficult to understand. One way to look at it is the idea of *maximum results with minimum input.* I've included 56 ways to leverage the concepts in this book, 56 levers representing the few vital philosophies and practices that you can use to move your life to a more outstanding level with a minimum of effort. I'm not saying it will all be easy, but rest assured that a lot of the heavy lifting has been done for you!

Even if you only use *one lever* consistently, you'll experience tremendous progress. However, if you consistently use *most* of the levers, you will experience exponential progress *in record time*. That's the power of compound leveraging!

The Four Parts of the Book, *Be. Do. Live.*

The 56 levers are divided into four logical groupings, as illustrated in the diagram above. This will make them easier for you to understand and apply:

1. **CREATE a compelling VISION.**
   The levers in this section will enable you to get absolute clarity on:
   - *What matters most to you and why?*
   - *Who would you be if you could be anyone? What would you do if everything were possible? How would you live if you were writing your life script?*
   - *How would you live if you only had limited time left?*

2. **ASSESS your current REALITY.**
   The levers in this section will help you begin answering the following questions:
   - *Are you intentionally living your life, or is life just happening to you?*
   - *Do you have a solid foundation for sustaining an outstanding quality of life?*
   - *What may be stopping you from being even more successful and even more fulfilled?*

3. **RE-IMAGINE your PHILOSOPHY.**
   The levers in this section will help you to understand:
   - *What are the vital few philosophies that make the biggest difference?*
   - *To what extent are you living in alignment with these philosophies?*
   - *How do you embed more empowering philosophies into your daily life?*

4. **OPTIMIZE your PRACTICES.**
   The levers in this section will help you to:
   - Recognize to what degree you're practicing the few things that make the biggest difference.
   - Act on the vital few practices that make the biggest difference.
   - Embed new practices to further enhance your quality of life.

As you can see, the book covers a lot of ground, but at the same time this rich personal journey is well mapped out for you.

A FEW FINAL THOUGHTS ON *BE. DO. LIVE.*

Before you jump in, let me offer you some suggestions for how you might approach reading the book.

- Remember, this is your life we're talking about, so don't just read *Be. Do. Live.* ONCE and then put it away. My suggestion is to keep this book near and revisit the material often, because I know each time you read the book you'll find more value.

- For some, the best option may be to read the book from beginning to end in a short period of time. For others, skimming through the book and selectively honing in on what most appeals may be the right approach. Choosing either of these two approaches, or anything in between, is fine!

- If there are any philosophies and/or practices that you find hard to relate to as you're reading, I suggest you keep moving and come back to these concepts at a later stage.

- As you reflect on what you've read, ask yourself this key question: *"How can I use this?"* By asking this question, you'll generate ideas for putting the various concepts into practice within your specific situation.

So pick the approach that works best for you personally. And congratulations on finding your way to the book and joining me on this exciting journey of discovery. I know that taking steps to live a more outstanding life will be fun and rewarding for you.

Let's get started!

CREATE A COMPELLING VISION

- What matters most to you and why?
- Who would you be if you could be anyone? What would you do if everything were possible? How would you live if you were writing your life script?
- How would you live if you only had limited time left?

WORDS *of* WISDOM

"Where there is no vision, the people perish."

PROVERBS 29:18

CHAPTER 1

How Would You Like to Be Remembered?

GET CLEAR ON YOUR DESIRED LEGACY

Have you ever thought about how you'd like to be remembered? Have you ever considered what you want your legacy to be?

I think it's fair to say that most of us don't really like to think about questions such as these. Why is this so? Perhaps we don't like thinking about our own death. Maybe we don't see any value in asking and answering such questions. Or could it be that we believe that there are other, more important things to focus on? No matter what the reasons are, reflecting on your mortality from time to time can serve a useful purpose.

Paulo Coelho, the best-selling author of *The Alchemist*, very elegantly summed up the value of reflecting on your mortality in his book *Like the Flowing River*: "*We are all walking towards death, but we never know when death will touch us and it is our duty, therefore, to look around us, to be grateful for each minute. But we should also be grateful to death, because it makes us think about the importance of each decision we take, or fail to take; it makes us stop doing anything that keeps us stuck in the category of the 'living dead' and, instead, urges us to risk everything, to bet everything on those things we always dreamed of doing, because, whether we like it or not, the angel of death is waiting for us.*"

By even starting to think about how you would like to be remembered after you're gone, you begin to consider how you want to live while you're still here. This reflection generates greater clarity about what's most important to you in the way you want to live. And having more clarity is the first essential step toward creating and sustaining a successful and fulfilling life.

It's tragic that many people go through their lives being unaware of and/or unaligned to what is most important to them and what they could consciously choose for themselves.

So let's not add to this tragic statistic. Instead, let's do an exercise that is designed to help you get more clarity about your vision for your life.

BOX SEAT AT YOUR FUNERAL

In your mind, fast-forward to your own funeral. Imagine that you are present there. And as you attend the service, assume that no one can see you (obviously!), but you can see, hear, and feel everything and everyone else. Picture this scene in your mind's eye as vividly as you can. And keeping this picture in mind, answer the following questions:

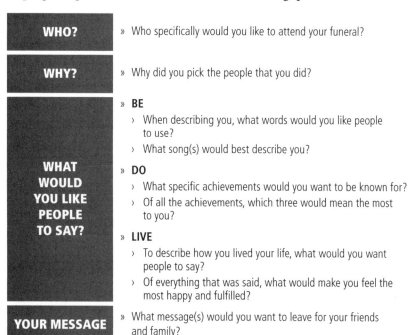

WHO?
» Who specifically would you like to attend your funeral?

WHY?
» Why did you pick the people that you did?

WHAT WOULD YOU LIKE PEOPLE TO SAY?
» **BE**
  › When describing you, what words would you like people to use?
  › What song(s) would best describe you?

» **DO**
  › What specific achievements would you want to be known for?
  › Of all the achievements, which three would mean the most to you?

» **LIVE**
  › To describe how you lived your life, what would you want people to say?
  › Of everything that was said, what would make you feel the most happy and fulfilled?

YOUR MESSAGE
» What message(s) would you want to leave for your friends and family?

How did you find the above exercise? Was it easy or was it hard? Did you experience any "Aha!" moments? What, if anything, became more obvious to you? Did you gain greater clarity about yourself and what you want your legacy to be?

At the very least, I do hope that the above hypothetical exercise got you to pause and reflect on the bigger picture. The fact is that we're all here for a finite period of time. And no one knows when the angel of death will touch us. So rather than waste any more time being stuck in the *"living dead"* category, let's take charge and move forward with purpose and passion.

WHAT NEXT?

With increased clarity about the vision for your life and your legacy, the next step is to assess the extent to which you are living the way you want to be remembered. Therefore, to make this assessment, answer the following two questions:

1. *On a scale of 1 to 10 (1 = not at all, 10 = totally), to what extent are you living in alignment with how you want to be remembered?*
2. *If you're not at level 10, what's the gap?*

If you are like most people, you will have a gap between your vision for your life/legacy and the way you are currently living. If that is the case for you, I recommend some further introspection. So take some time to review and answer the following questions:

- *What is most important to you?*
- *What does "lasting success" mean to you?*
- *To be more aligned with the way you want to be remembered . . .*
  - *Who do you need to be?*
  - *What do you need to do?*
  - *How do you need to live?*

The key message is *don't postpone your best life.* Don't wait for a wake-up call before you reach for more for yourself. Don't wait till you're dying to really start living.

Instead, commit to taking the necessary steps so that you can live more in harmony with the vision you have for your life and your legacy.

WORDS *of* WISDOM

"Whatever you need to do and want to do,
do it today.
There are only so many tomorrows."

ANONYMOUS

CHAPTER 2

What Is a Must for You to Experience?

WHAT IS LIFE?

When you take a broad view of it, life is really a series of experiences—experiences of different sizes, shapes, and colors, to speak metaphorically. For example, the experience of:

- Feeling the cool breeze on a hot summer day
- Witnessing a glorious sunset
- Holding a toddler in your arms, feeling awed by the miracle of life
- Witnessing a nail-biting finish at a sporting contest
- Enjoying a memorable kiss
- Achieving a professional goal that you so badly wanted
- Watching fireworks at a beautiful setting, whether in a big city or in the countryside
- Sipping a frozen margarita at the Hilton Waikoloa Village in Kona, Hawaii (one of the best places that I've ever visited!)
- and so on

Wouldn't you agree that there is no limit to what we could experience in our lifetime? Would you also agree that the opportunities to experience what we want have never been better, compared to 20, 10, or even 5 years ago? What do I mean by that? Let me share a quick personal example.

In the late '80s, I was studying for my degree in London. My parents, at that time, were living in India. Talking to my parents was something I really looked forward to every week. However, the phone calls from the U.K. to India were rather expensive—as best I can remember, around four dollars per minute. And therefore, being on a tight student budget, the length of time I could talk to them had to be rationed. I distinctly remember having a phone in one hand and a watch in the other to make sure I didn't exceed the amount of time that I could afford. Contrast this situation to what I have today. Thanks to technology advancements, I can be on Skype every day, for several hours, talking with friends and family across the globe, without having to pay a single cent!

So, all in all, we are living in amazing times where:

- There is so much we can experience, and
- The opportunities have never been better.

Yet, the puzzling and disappointing thing is that most people fail to experience what they really want in their lifetime. Why is this so?

There are two key reasons:

1. **Lack of clarity.** People don't take the time to define, and then plan, what they want to experience. They never consciously ask and answer the question: *"What do I want to experience, and when?"*

2. **Lack of urgency.** Even if they are clear in their own mind about what they want to experience, people tend to procrastinate. They adhere to the notion: *"There is always tomorrow. I have other, more important priorities right now."*

At this point, you might also be thinking of a third reason: Lack of resources—time, money, energy, and so on. For example, you may be asking: *Don't you need time and money to travel?* Yes, I do agree that time and money are important. However, I also believe that when you're clear on what you want to experience and have a sense of urgency, there are many ways to attract the money and find the time. For some reason, we can always find time and money for things that are important to us. Time and money are often convenient excuses for why we aren't experiencing something—however, more often than not, it's not a lack of resources, but *a lack of resourcefulness* that gets in the way.

HOW TO CREATE YOUR DESIRED EXPERIENCES

The solution is twofold:
1. **Be clear** about what you want to experience.
2. Attach a sense of **urgency** to creating your desired experiences.

So how do you do that? Let me illustrate, using the diagram below. On the horizontal X-axis is the **"Time Left to Live"** (to create a sense of urgency, I've used from three months to five years) and on the vertical Y-axis are the **"Desired Experiences."**

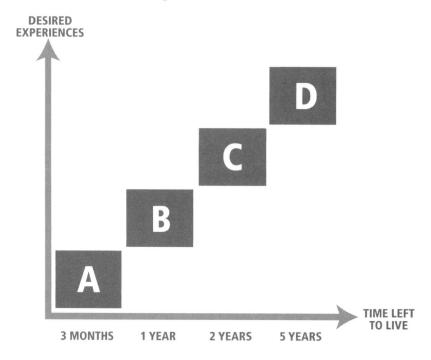

Each of the above boxes (A, B, C, D) represents the experiences you want to have at that related point in time. For each period, write down your answers to the following questions:

1. **Box A:** *If I only had three months to live, what would I want to experience?*
2. **Box B:** *If I only had one year to live, what else would I want to experience?*
3. **Box C:** *If I only had two years to live, what else would I want to experience?*
4. **Box D:** *If I only had five years to live, what else would I want to experience?*

This exercise may be simple, but it's not easy. This is because it forces you to think long and hard about what's most important for you to experience and then to prioritize your desired experiences against an immovable deadline: your own mortality! But this exercise is definitely worth doing, because it will give you both clarity and some sense of urgency. And with increased clarity and urgency, you are more likely to take the actions necessary to create your desired experiences.

WORDS *of* WISDOM

"The more clear your vision of health, happiness,
and prosperity, the faster you move toward
it and the faster it moves toward you."

BRIAN TRACY
Peak Performance Coach, Best-Selling Author

CHAPTER 3

Do You Have a Design for Your Life?

DESIGN VS. DEFAULT

There are two ways you can live your life. You can either live by design or you can live by default. Let me explain what I mean.

Living by design is when you live life on your own terms. The ABCs of living by design are:

- When you feel that you are the **A**RCHITECT of your life
- When you have a **B**LUEPRINT for your life
- When you **C**ONSTRUCT your life according to your blueprint

Living by default, on the other hand, is when you don't live life on your own terms. Instead, you live a life that is at the mercy of circumstances and/or the desires of other people. You feel that your life is not aligned with what's important to you. You feel as if you're just going through the motions without your life having much meaning. You feel like you're doing things because you **have to** rather than because you **want to** do them.

When you live by default, the best you can hope for is a moderate amount of success and fulfillment, and at worst, a continued sense of helplessness, frustration, and dissatisfaction.

Living by design is the only real path to sustainable success and fulfillment. And therefore, for obvious reasons, I recommend *living by design*.

WHAT ABOUT YOU?

How are you currently living? Is it mostly by design or is it mostly by default? You may instinctively know the answer to my question. Or you may not be sure. Either way, to get more clarity as to where you sit, take a few minutes to answer the following few questions.

On a scale of 1 to 10, with 1 being *not at all,* and 10 being *totally,* to what extent . . .

1. *Do you feel that you are in charge of your own life?*
2. *Do you feel that you consciously choose how you respond to people and events?*
3. *Are you clear about your purpose in life?*
4. *Do you have clarity about what "lasting success" means to you?* (More on this coming up soon.)
5. *Have you documented (written about, journaled on, etc.) your purpose in life and what "lasting success" means to you?*
6. *Do you choose your goals in line with your definition of "lasting success"?*
7. *Are your being, doing, and living aligned with your life's purpose?*

Add up your scores. How did you do? Would you agree that unless you scored a perfect 70, there is room for improvement? Assuming this to be the case, let's do some further exploring.

LIVING BY DESIGN

As stated previously, the ABCs of living by design are:

- When you feel that you are the **A**RCHITECT of your life
- When you have a **B**LUEPRINT for your life
- When you **C**ONSTRUCT your life according to your blueprint

I'm going to make an assumption before proceeding further. And this is that the A of the ABCs is already taken care of, i.e., you absolutely *know* that you are the architect of your own life. Because if you didn't feel this way, you wouldn't be reading this book. But perhaps NOW is the time to become more active in this role.

At the outset, let me also state that living by design is not an event. Instead, it's a journey. It's a continual process, just as life is.

With the above assumptions in play, let's look at the B & C of living by design.

Having a BLUEPRINT for your life

You may be wondering, *"What exactly is a 'blueprint' for my life?"* So let's answer this. Your life blueprint is an articulation of two key elements:

1. Your Life Purpose Statement (LPS)
2. Your definition of "lasting success"

Let's review each of the above items in turn, and also go through an exercise to develop each element of your life's blueprint.

1. Develop a Life Purpose Statement.

A Life Purpose Statement (or LPS) is your articulation (in words, sentences, pictures, paragraphs, etc.) of what you believe you are here on this planet for.

As an example, here's what Rose Fitzgerald Kennedy, mother of John F. Kennedy, saw as her purpose in life: *"To raise a family of world leaders."* Closer to home, my purpose in life is: *"To radiate god's love, presence, and playfulness in serving myself and others on our guided paths."*

You may be thinking: *"But I don't know what my life purpose is. How do I discover what it is? What if I don't get it right?"* Please don't sweat this. Developing an LPS may feel like a daunting exercise. But trust me, there is no way to get this *wrong,* and if you currently don't have a Life

Purpose Statement, you can't go backwards anyway. At this point, the aim of developing an LPS is not to write it down perfectly, but instead to come up with a rough draft. Refining and evolving your LPS is not necessarily a quick process. It may take days, weeks, or even months. So rest assured, it's perfectly fine to get something down as a first draft, and build on it later. So let's get started.

In the first chapter, you imagined a vision for your life, a vision of how you would like to be remembered. So take some time to review what you imagined. And as you do that, write down answers to the following questions:

- *What are some of the most important elements in your vision for your life?*
- *What are some recurring patterns?*
- *What elements of being, doing, and living are most important to you?*

As you review your answers to the above, identify the common themes that emerge for you. How could you articulate the most important elements? Now have a go at writing your LPS, by completing the following sentence:

"The purpose of my life is . . . "

As you finish the above sentence, I urge you to not censor your answers. Don't judge. Just *go for it!* Keep writing until you have exhausted all your ideas.

2. Define "lasting success."

The word "success" can mean different things to different people. For some, success is primarily about money, e.g., making $100 million a year. For others, success is principally about family, e.g., raising a loving family. For still others, success is foremost about spirituality, e.g., developing and maintaining a high level of spiritual connection with their creator. And then for yet others, success is about all or none of the above. There is no right or wrong answer, per se. The problem arises when we use other people's definition of success to determine whether or not we are successful.

To avoid this mistake, it's necessary to spell out in detail what "lasting success" means to you. Prior to doing so, though, review the following tips:

- Define "lasting success" for all areas. Lasting success needs to be considered across all areas of life. From my perspective, for example, succeeding in your professional life at the expense of your relationships is not lasting success. So my recommendation is that you define what lasting success means *for you* across all aspects of your life, including:
  - › Physical health and vitality
  - › Financial security and freedom
  - › Career, work, job, mission, business
  - › Intimate relationships
  - › Other relationships
  - › Emotional health
  - › Role in the community
  - › Spiritual life

- Consider all elements of being, doing, and living. Very often, success is defined in the context of doing only, i.e., accomplishments and achievements. That is a very narrow definition of what success is all about. My recommendation is that in defining lasting success, you consider all three elements of being, doing, and living.

OK, let's begin to define "lasting success." As a first step, review your Life Purpose Statement, and the thinking leading up to that point.

With the above as input, work through each of your life areas in turn. Ask yourself questions that will allow you to crystallize what "lasting success" really means to you. Questions such as:

- *What is my ultimate vision for this area of my life?*
- *Who do I aspire to be in this area?*
- *What do I want to do?*
- *How do I want to live?*
- *If I had already reached the point where I want to be, how would that look and feel?*
- *What words and/or images best capture my vision?*

Capture your answers to the above—whether that be in words, pictures, and in any other way that has meaning for you. As mentioned above, make sure you develop your definition of "lasting success" across all your life areas.

CONSTRUCT your life

Having a blueprint for your life, on paper, is also important. However, the real value is when you embody the essence of your blueprint and use it to guide your behavior on a day-to-day basis. That's what constructing your life based on your blueprint means.

At a practical level, it means that you use your life blueprint as a compass to . . .

- Set your short-term and longer-term goals.
- Develop your monthly and weekly plans.
- Consciously choose your daily habits of being, doing, and living.

Most of all, you need to be strong in the hard moments. What do I mean? I mean that you'll want to show resilience when your buttons are pushed, and you have to choose between default and design.

A final note on your blueprint—it's not a static thing. As you evolve, your blueprint will evolve accordingly. As a minimum, I suggest that you review your blueprint once a year.

W O R D S *of* W I S D O M

"The best and most beautiful things
in the world cannot be seen nor even
touched, but just felt in the heart."

H E L E N K E L L E R
(1880–1968)
American Author, Activist, and Lecturer

CHAPTER 4

What Is Your Real Target?

WHAT IF YOU HAD A MAGIC WAND?

Imagine that you have a magic wand able to instantly fulfill any of your desires. Now get ready to answer this question: *"What would you like this magic wand to give you?"*

I invite you to pause, grab a pen and paper, and answer the above question.

OK, what did you write? Did your wish list include any of the following?

- More money
- Fulfilling relationships
- Travel to exotic places
- Profitable business
- More time
- Energy and vitality
- Empowering boss
- Rewarding career

People often include these items on their wish lists. It's fine if your list also included other things. But what if I told you that what you really want is something else entirely . . .

FIVE WHYs

In a minute, I'm going to help you work through a process that will allow you to get a deeper perspective about what you and I are really after. To do so, I'm going to assume **more money** was on your list. If it wasn't, I suggest that you still follow the exercise below and answer the following questions in order to get acquainted with the process:

1. *Why do you want more money?* Make a list of your answers (capture your responses in a list and label it as List 1).
2. Review List 1 and for each item on it, ask yourself: *Why do I want this?* Again, make a list of your answers (label this as List 2).
3. Review List 2 and for each item on List 2, ask yourself: *Why do I want this?* Again, make a list of your answers (label this as List 3).
4. Review List 3 and for each item on List 3, ask yourself: *Why do I want this?* Again, make a list of your answers (label this as List 4).
5. Review List 4 and for each item on List 4, ask yourself: *Why do I want this?* Again, make a list of your answers (label this as List 5).

Keep repeating the above steps until you reach a *"dead end,"* i.e., until you reach a point where you aren't coming up with anything new and hear yourself repeating the same answers.

Here's a simple example of answers to the above exercise to make it even more clear.

- First QUESTION: *Why do I want more money?*
  - ANSWER: Because I want a bigger house.
- Next QUESTION: *Why do I want a bigger house?*
  - ANSWER: Because I want more space.
- Next QUESTION: *Why do I want more space?*
  - ANSWER: Because it gives me a sense of freedom.

So for the simple example on the previous page, here's what the different lists would look like summarized:

List 1	List 2	List 3
Bigger house	Space	Sense of freedom

OK, review what you came up with. Compare your List 1 with List 5, or even List 4, List 3 or List 2. What's the difference? What do you observe? Do you notice that as you go deeper (i.e., from List 1 to List 2, and so on), you start hitting the real reasons as to why you want more money?

I can understand if you find this exercise annoying, but it does serve a purpose. When you've completed the exercise, I hope you'll come to some of the following conclusions:

1. You are not after money for money's sake (i.e., you're not a collector of pieces of paper with faces of dead people printed on them).
2. What you're after is what money can provide for you (e.g., a bigger house, more space, a sense of freedom, and so on).
3. The real reasons you want more money are revealed at the deeper level (e.g., money gives you a sense of freedom).

If money was not on your wish list and/or you're still not convinced, go ahead and pick something else from your list. Go through the FIVE WHYs exercise again.

No matter what you pick from your wish list, let me predict the outcome now. My prediction is that if you continue to explore the *"Why"* enough times, and at a deeper level every time, you'll come to the following conclusion:

What I am *really* after is a FEELING.

Secure, free, adventurous, peaceful, happy—these are all examples of feelings. So one could argue that, at the deepest level, what we're really after is to feel a certain way.

Even if you agree with what I'm saying, you may be thinking: *"Does that mean that I shouldn't strive for more money, better health, fulfilling relationships, etc.?"*

My answer is: *"Absolutely not—that isn't what I mean at all!"* So what do I mean by all of this? By having greater clarity about the feelings you want to experience, you broaden your options regarding how you can go about experiencing those feelings. For example, by asking certain types of questions, you may find yourself exploring options that you previously had ignored. Questions such as:

- *Who can I be to feel more <insert you target feelings>?*
- *What can I do to feel more <insert your target feelings>?*
- *How can I live to feel more <insert your target feelings>?*

YOUR TARGET FEELINGS

If feelings are what we're really after, I hope you will agree that it makes sense to get really clear on what our *target set of feelings* is. To do so, pause for some reflection and introspection, and answer the following questions:

1. *What feelings are most important for you to experience on a consistent basis?*
2. *What feelings do you most want to avoid?*
3. *What feelings do you normally feel on a regular basis?*
4. *Where do you have a gap?*

Now that you know where your gaps are, what do you believe are some options for addressing them?

W O R D S *of* W I S D O M

"When you are inspired by some great purpose,
some extraordinary project, all your thoughts
break their bonds. Your mind transcends
limitations, your consciousness expands and you
find yourself in a great and wonderful world.
You discover yourself to be a greater person."

PATANJALI
a Foremost Indian Scholar,
who lived around the 2nd or 3rd century C.E.

CHAPTER 5

What Is Your BHAG?

WHAT'S A BHAG?

The term "BHAG" (pronounced "bee-hag") stands for **Big Hairy Audacious Goal** ("**BHAG**"). It was a term coined by authors Jim Collins and Jerry I. Porras in their book *Built to Last*, which examines the qualities of successful visionary companies. They found that the one factor separating successful efforts from unsuccessful ones was the use of ambitious, even outrageous, goals to inspire people and focus toward specific accomplishments.

BHAG is just as applicable on an individual level as it is at a team or organizational level. On an individual level, I think of BHAG as a goal that is so big, so huge, that it appears far out of reach and almost impossible to achieve. If actually accomplished, even in small part, this goal would thrill you to no end and would most likely make a huge impact on society.

WHY SET A BHAG?

Perhaps a better question is: *"Why **not** set a BHAG?"*

In setting and striving toward a BHAG, three things are certain:

1. It will stretch you far beyond your comfort zone.
2. It will force you to think radically.
3. It will cause you to grow beyond your wildest imagination.

My BHAG is to positively impact two billion people during my lifetime. When I think of my BHAG, on one hand I feel very excited, and on the other it seems so totally out of reach. But one thing is certain: It makes me ask much broader and far bigger questions. The book that you now hold in your hands is a result of the questions I asked myself during the process of deciding how to make progress toward my BHAG.

You may be wondering: *What if I don't accomplish my BHAG?*

It is more than likely that most of us won't fully achieve our BHAG. But so what? Jim Rohn, best-selling author and a popular motivational speaker, advises that *"You should set a goal big enough that in the process of achieving it, you become something worth becoming."* The purpose of a goal, especially a BHAG, is not necessarily to achieve the actual goal but to expand who you become while *pursuing* the goal. I know this sounds contradictory; however, the real goal and ultimate reward in the pursuit of a BHAG is *the expanded person that you become* during the quest.

IDENTIFY YOUR BHAG(S)

Now it's your turn. Are you ready to have a go at identifying your BHAG(s)? Here's a process I suggest:

1. **Review.** Analyze your outputs from the previous chapters. Specifically, the following:
   - *How would you like to be remembered?*
   - Your Life Purpose Statement (LPS)
   - Your definition of "lasting success"

2. **Examine.** What should be the criteria for a BHAG? On his website, Jim Collins poses the question: *"Do you have a good BHAG or bad BHAG?"* He further goes on to define the five criteria of a good BHAG. He says that good BHAGs:

- Are set with understanding, not bravado
- Fit squarely in the intersection between the following three criteria:
  - What you are deeply passionate about
  - What you could be "best in the world" at
  - What drives your economic engine
- Have a long time frame—10 to 30 years
- Are clear, compelling, and easy to grasp
- Directly reflect your core values and core purpose

3. **Visualize.** Think about your possible answers to the following questions:
   - *What is a great purpose that inspires you?*
   - *What is an extraordinary project that's compelling to you?*
   - *What are some outrageous goals that you haven't even considered because they feel so impossible to achieve?*
   - *What are goals that could make a lasting contribution to millions of others?*
   - *What is something that you are deeply passionate about?*
   - *If you could be world-class at something, what would that be?*

4. **Write.** For the next 5 minutes, find as many ways as you can to finish the sentence *"My BHAG is . . . "*

5. **Select.** Of all the goals you wrote in the previous step, select the one(s) that excite you the most—and at the same time, scare you the most.

BHAGs are fun to have because they create excitement in our lives. It's easier to get inspired by a big goal than a small step, even though both can be important in making progress. So go ahead and let yourself be inspired by a BIG dream, your own personal BHAG.

ASSESS YOUR CURRENT REALITY

- Are you intentionally living your life, or is life just happening to you?
- Do you have a solid foundation for sustaining an outstanding quality of life?
- What may be stopping you from being even more successful and even more fulfilled?

W O R D S *of* W I S D O M

"Who you think you are does not have the
capacity to realize the truth of who you are . . .
Who you truly are can recognize this. You have
the right to recognize this. It is nothing that
anyone can give you or take away from you. It
can be veiled by the powers of the mind, but a
veil does not really cover anything . . . What lies
behind the veil is the truth of your essential self.
The veil is simply your latest self-definition."

G A N G A J I
Author of *The Diamond in Your Pocket*

CHAPTER 6

Who Are You?

WHO AM I?

This is perhaps the most profound question that you could ever ask yourself. It is not an easy one to answer though. For thousands of years, great saints, philosophers, and intellectuals have pondered this question. And in spite of the extensive focus on this question over such a long period of time, there is no universally accepted answer.

Though it's not an easy question to answer, it is an important one to consider. This is because whatever you believe to be the answer to this question will, to a great extent, determine the quality of your life.

So, before continuing, pause for a moment and ask yourself:

- *Who am I?*
- *Who am I, really?*

Keep asking and answering some more questions, such as:

- *Who else am I?*
- *How do I know that is who I am?*

Well, what were your answers to the above questions? To what extent were your answers based on one or more of the following:

- The **roles** you play (e.g., father, mother, wife, husband, brother, sister, son, etc.)
- Your **profession** (e.g., lawyer, teacher, CEO, etc.)
- Your **possessions** (e.g., millionaire, homeowner, business owner, etc.)
- Your **qualities** (e.g., kind, loving, generous, patient, adventurous, determined, decisive, etc.)
- Your **gender** (male or female)
- Your **nationality** (American, Australian, Irish, Italian, etc.)

Now imagine for a minute that you can't refer to any of the above attributes (i.e., roles, profession, possessions, etc.) in answering the *"Who am I?"* question. With this new constraint, again ask yourself: *Who am I?*

THE TWO CHOICES

At the highest level, there are two fundamental ways to reframe the *"Who am I?"* question:

1. *Am I a human being having a spiritual experience?*

or

2. *Am I a spiritual being having a human experience?*

My belief is that we are all spiritual beings having a human experience. What this means is that there is so much **more** to us than what we can see and experience—we are all **more** than the roles we play, our profession, our possessions, our qualities, and so on. In a nutshell, we are **more** than our personalities.

But what is this **more** that I am referring to above? The **more** is something that words can't accurately describe—words can only serve as pointers or signposts.

This **more** is the constant and unchanging reality that makes the human experience possible. This **more** is our consciousness; it is our higher self; it is the Divine within us; it is our ultimate awareness.

In Indian philosophy, **more** is referred to as ***Atman.*** A. Parthasarathy, in his best-selling book, *Vedanta Treatise,* provides an excellent overview of the relationship between ***Atman*** and our body, mind, and intellect.

"You are Atman appearing as an individual. Atman is omnipresent. It is like the sun whose rays are all-pervading. There is just one sun above. But wherever there is a reflecting surface there appears in it a reflected sun, an individual sun. The reflecting sun assumes the properties of the reflecting medium. The sun seen through a blue mirror appears blue. The sun seen through a dirty mirror appears dirty, through a broken mirror, broken and so on. But the sun above is immaculate and unconditioned by the qualities of the reflecting media. Similarly there is just one all-pervading Atman. But wherever there is a body-mind-intellect equipment, Atman appears through it as an individual human being. The individual takes to the properties of his body, mind and intellect but not Atman. Atman remains ever pure and uncontaminated like the sun vis-à-vis its images."

The more intensely you believe that this consciousness or higher self or Divine within is the real you, the more power, peace, and happiness you will experience.

As Oprah Winfrey once said, *"It isn't until you come to a spiritual understanding of who you are—not necessarily a religious feeling, but deep down, the spirit within—that you can begin to take control."*

WORDS *of* WISDOM

"To master your life, you must master your
emotions. To master your emotions, you
must become a master of meaning."

ANTHONY ROBBINS
Best-Selling Author, Peak Performance Coach

CHAPTER 7

What Controls Your Life?

MEANING

All human beings share the same nervous system design—a system of cells, tissues, and organs that regulates the body's responses to internal and external stimuli. Even though we all share the same design, individuals will still respond differently to the same stimulus or trigger. Why?

The reason we respond differently is because we give **different meanings** to the same stimulus or trigger. At a basic level, the meaning we give is whether something is good or bad or neutral. And then the meaning we assign to the stimulus, in turn, drives our individual behavior. Next, our behavior dictates the results we get. The following diagram sums up these concepts.

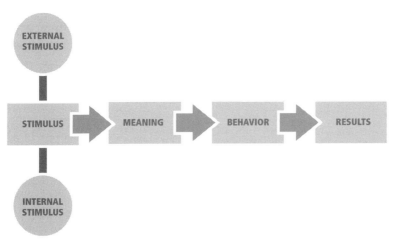

Since all of this is true, it means that if we want different results in our lives, we need to behave differently. And in order to behave differently, we need to change the meaning we give to the stimulus. So the million-dollar questions are:

1. *How do you create meaning?*
2. *How do you change the meaning you give?*

HOW DO YOU CREATE MEANING?

The meaning you give to triggers at any point in time is determined by your **Stimulus Evaluation System (SES).** Your SES creates meaning in response to both internal stimulus (your thoughts) and external stimulus (people, events).

Your SES is made up of six elements: mood, motive, beliefs, values, expectations, and fears. These six elements act as an integrated automatic filter through which we assess stimulus and form the meaning. Let's briefly review each of the six elements.

1. **Mood.** Your mood or emotional state at any moment influences the way you behave at that time. When you're in an angry mood, for example, no matter what the trigger, you're more likely to react in an angry manner.

2. **Motive.** Your motives are your real reasons for doing something. You may or may not be aware of your real motives in a particular situation. Even if you are aware of your motives, you may not share your motives with others. This is sometimes referred to in the corporate environment as your *hidden agenda.* You can uncover your real motives in any situation by asking yourself the following questions:

- *What is really driving me?*
- *What is the outcome I really want?*
- *What is it that I want to experience and/or avoid experiencing?*

3. **Beliefs.** A belief is something that you accept as true about something or someone. We have beliefs about ourselves, other people, life, relationships, work, spirituality, finances, situations, and so on. And what we believe is an integral component in how we evaluate stimulus and assign meaning.

4. **Values.** A value is something that is important to you. Values can exist at multiple levels, including categories, activities, and feelings.

   - Examples of categories: family, spirituality, health, career, growth, etc.
   - Examples of specific activities: playing with children, solving complex problems, reading literature, exercising, etc.
   - Examples of specific feelings: joy, adventurous, free, important, secure, etc.

5. **Expectations.** Your expectations about events, people, and even yourself play a huge part in the meaning you assign to any given situation and how you respond to it. All disappointment is in fact a result of unmet expectations.

6. **Fears.** It's natural for us to avoid what we fear, and as such our fears influence how we assign meaning and respond to stimulus.

The following diagram takes into account the SES to present a more refined version of the previous diagram.

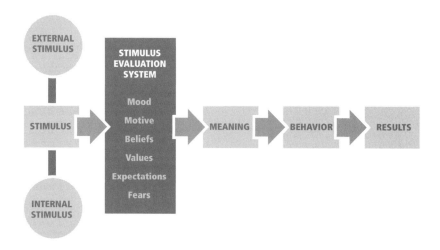

HOW DO YOU CHANGE THE MEANINGS YOU GIVE?

To change the meaning you give to a stimulus, you must first become conscious of your SES. However, most of us don't really know about our SES. This is because:

1. Our SES is dynamic. It evolves over the course of our lives as we subconsciously form habitual patterns of mood, motives, beliefs, values, expectations, and fears. Both nature and nurture play a big part in shaping our SES.
2. Our SES often exists at a subconscious level.
3. We don't take time to become aware of our SES.

To understand your SES, the first step is therefore to examine your habitual moods, motives, beliefs, values, expectations, and fears.

Once you are aware of your SES, the next step is to assess the extent to which it may be limiting your life. And only then can you decide what changes you want to make.

Some of the actions I have taken to enhance my Stimulus Evaluation System include:

- Learning techniques that enable me to quickly change my mood
- Being more honest about my intentions and true motives
- Expanding my identity by doing things that I wouldn't normally do
- Changing beliefs that no longer serve me
- Becoming more aware of my expectations
- Acknowledging my fears and then taking action to overcome them

What are some of the steps you want to explore for improving your own Stimulus Evaluation System (SES)?

WORDS *of* WISDOM

"Achieving a balanced life is a choice that each
of us continually makes second by second,
thought by thought, feeling by feeling. On the
one hand we can simply exist. But on the other,
we can choose to pack out seconds and create
valuable minutes in all aspects of our lives."

MARK VICTOR HANSEN
Author, *Chicken Soup for the Soul*

CHAPTER 8

How Aligned Is Your Wheel of Life?

ARE YOU A JUGGLER?

Most of us are jugglers. We are busy juggling multiple areas of our lives—career, family, finances, relationships, health, and so on. And often while some areas of our lives are going well (e.g., work, health), there will be other areas that are not doing so great (e.g., relationships, finances). A common challenge for most of us is to find the optimum balance in life.

The challenge of finding the right balance is often magnified for three reasons:

1. We are not clear on what we want and why we want it.
2. We are unsure about the relative priorities of things that are important to us.
3. We don't regularly measure our progress. (Keep in mind that the phrase *"You can't improve what you don't measure"* applies universally to all areas of life.)

WHAT IS YOUR SITUATION?

What about you? How balanced is your life? To make this assessment, I recommend that you do the following exercise. You'll need paper and a pen or pencil.

1. The diagram below represents a generic "Wheel of Life" and indicates areas of life that typically are important to people (e.g., physical, financial, work). Review the categories to ensure that the generic Wheel of Life works for you. Feel free to delete and/or add areas according to what is important to you.

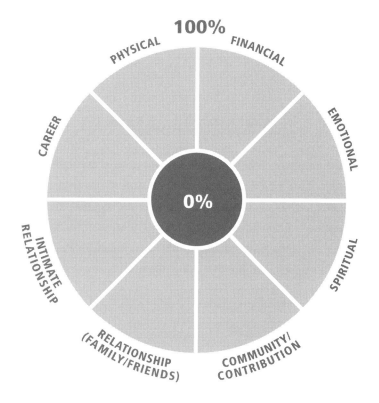

2. Pick a time horizon that you want to use (e.g., 6 months, 12 months, 3 years, etc). For each category on your Wheel of Life, write down what success would look like for you in that area, within your chosen time horizon.

3. Ask yourself: *"If 100% is where I really want to be (within my chosen timeframe), where am I now?"* Then, for each category on your Wheel of Life, draw an arc that represents your current status. For example, if you feel that you're only at 50% of your ideal financial status right

now, draw an arched line halfway between the outer and inner ring inside the "financial" pie slice.

4. Connect the eight arcs to create a single shape. This shape is your current Wheel of Life (you may want to shade it in for added emphasis).

5. Review your Wheel of Life, and answer the following questions:

   - *Were you pleasantly surprised or massively shocked by the final shape?*
   - *If this wheel were attached to your car of life, how would the ride be? Would it be a smooth ride or a bumpy experience?*

HOW TO MAKE PROGRESS

If you're like most people, your Wheel of Life may need some alignment. Well, going through the following three-step process will enable you to make progress.

1. **Create urgency.**

   - *What areas of your life need more attention?*
   - *What has it cost you in the past to have ignored aspects of your life? What might it cost you in the future if you don't do anything differently?*
   - *What would dramatically improve if you made changes?*

- *On a scale of 1 to 10 (1 = not at all, 10 = totally), how committed are you to making the necessary changes? If not at level 10, what would need to happen for you to be totally committed?*

2. **Decide.**

- *What are the few changes that would make the biggest difference?*
- *What could you stop and/or start and/or continue to do?*
- *What are some decisions that you are totally committed to following through?*

3. **Take action.**

- *What actions will you take in the next day/week/month?*
- *Who could you share your decisions and actions with, someone who could support you and/or hold you accountable to follow through?*
- *How could you monitor your progress?*

You can turn to the Wheel of Life time and time again to see how you're doing in the important areas of your life. I think you'll find it to be a helpful tool for getting an insightful overview. Then use the three-step process described above to make the desired improvements.

WORDS *of* WISDOM

"You don't have any problems.
You only THINK that you do."

A COURSE IN MIRACLES

CHAPTER 9

Is Perspective the Biggest Problem You Have?

THE PROBLEM OF PERSPECTVE

Think about a problem that is really bothering you at this moment. Once you've thought about such a problem, answer this question: *On a scale of 1 to 10 (1 = not at all, 10 = a lot), how much is this problem bothering you?* If you answered 7 or less, then I suggest that you pick a problem that is at level 8 or above. Once you've thought of something at level 8 or above, please read on.

Now imagine you are told, at this very moment, that you are going to die in less than a month. I know this is just a hypothetical exercise, but let this new fact really sink in, as if it were true.

Once again, pause and ask yourself: *"To what extent is the problem that I identified bothering me now?"* I predict with 100% certainty that your score will be much lower than it was a minute ago!

You may at this instant be thinking: *"Yes, that is true, but what's the point?"* Here's my point. The reason your problem isn't bothering you as much now as it did before is because, in light of the new information (imminent death), your perspective on the problem has changed. In contrast to imminent death, your original problem is not a big deal.

The great Greek philosopher Socrates captured the essence of this type of change in perspective very skillfully when he said, *"If all our misfortunes were laid in one common heap, whence everyone must take an equal portion, most people would be content to take their own and depart."* In other words, in comparison to *all* the possible problems that we could have, our own challenges seem much more acceptable.

The reason that many situations seem like problems to us is because we don't view these situations from the appropriate perspective. And so when we do alter our perspective, we can change the way we feel about the problem. As Dr. Wayne Dyer, best-selling author and popular speaker, puts it: *"When you change the way you look at things, the things you look at change."*

Therefore, in essence, the **biggest problem** we all have is a **problem of perspective**.

HOW DO YOU CHANGE YOUR PERSPECTIVE?

How do you alter your perspective on an issue or a problem? One of the most effective ways is to ask yourself a simple, but powerful question when facing a problem or an issue. And that question is:

> *"In the grand scheme of things, will this incident/issue/ problem matter a year from now, or a decade from now?"*

By pausing to reflect in this way, you force yourself to get a helicopter view of the situation. And when you view the situation from a higher vantage point, you're more than likely to change your perspective, or at the very least, lower your emotional intensity about the situation. This reduced emotional intensity results in a clearer headspace, a place from which you are better able to develop an effective action plan for confronting and resolving the issue.

Some other approaches to help alter your perspective are outlined below:

1. **Get clarity.** Sometimes a lack of beneficial information causes us to jump in our thinking to the worst-case scenarios. To avoid this, ask yourself:
   - *Could I be misunderstanding the situation?*
   - *Are the assumptions that I'm making correct? How can I be 100% sure?*

2. **Check for an overreaction.** At times, we make a bigger deal out of something than it really is. To determine if this is the case, ask yourself:
   - *Am I overreacting?*
   - *Am I making more of this than is necessary?*

3. **Look for the gift and the opportunity.** Napoleon Hill, in his famous book *Think and Grow Rich,* said, "Every adversity carries within it a seed of equal or greater opportunity," a restatement of the saying "every cloud has a silver lining."

   To uncover the potential gift in any situation, ask yourself:
   - *What is the gift that might be disguised in this problem?*
   - *How can this problem/situation provide me with an opportunity to grow even more?* (Every problem is an opportunity to grow if you choose to believe it.)

4. **Look beyond the problem.** Instead of focusing on the problem, imagine and anticipate the positive emotions you'll feel once you've resolved the problem.

I think you'll now see that changing your perspective is very possible!

The following quote from Allen Neuharth, the businessman who founded the most widely read newspaper in the United States, *USA Today,* sums up the essence of this chapter.

> *"The difference between a mountain
> and a molehill is your perspective."*

Bring this quote to mind at times when you sense you need to tweak your perspective and return to this chapter for assistance in the process.

WORDS *of* WISDOM

"Seek not outside yourself, for all pain simply
comes from a futile search for what you
want, insisting where it must be found."

A COURSE IN MIRACLES

CHAPTER 10

What Is the Source of All Your Pain?

WHAT CAUSES PAIN?

All of us have experienced painful emotions at some stage in our lives. And when we experience such feelings, one of the things we do is to look for the reasons or causes of our pain. In doing so, we sometimes incorrectly blame other people and circumstances for the pain we feel.

Irrespective of what might seem to cause you pain, at the most fundamental level, the ultimate source of all pain is the same—**the non-acceptance of what is**.

So what do I mean by "what is"? It is whatever is showing up in this moment, this very instant. And that *what is* can be anything—a thought, a feeling, a sensation, an action, an experience, another person, or a specific event.

If we unconditionally accept whatever is showing up right now, then there is no resistance. And when there is no resistance, there is no pain.

Think about your life. Think of any number of situations where you have experienced pain in the past. For any of these situations, answer this question: *"Did you unconditionally accept what was showing up in that moment?"* My sense is that your answer to this question would be a resounding NO.

Now, even if you agree with my observations, you may also be thinking: *"But if I always accept what is, how can I ever make any progress? Won't this make me apathetic? Wouldn't it cause me to lose my drive? Wouldn't it allow other people to get away with inappropriate behavior?"*

THE PARADOX

If you're thinking along the lines stated above, I can understand where you're coming from; that's because I also believe that **all progress comes from non-acceptance of what is.** For example, think about all the progress that human beings have made, all the discoveries, all the inventions, etc. Do you think any of these would have been possible if we had simply accepted whatever the situation was?

This leads to an interesting **paradox,** which is that:

> **All pain comes from non-acceptance of what is**
> **AND**
> **All progress also comes from non-acceptance of what is.**

HOW TO LIVE THE PARADOX

The first step in living the paradox is to be aware of it. Being aware is a big part of the solution. Having said that, however, there is no foolproof solution—no silver bullet to dealing completely with this paradox. So let me share something with you. There is a process that I have personally found useful in dealing with this paradox. It is outlined below:

1. When I find myself resisting whatever is showing up, I pause, take a deep breath, and remind myself: *"That's just the way it is."*

2. With a sense of acceptance, I then review the current situation and:
   - Clarify my desired outcome *("What is the result I want?").*
   - Assess the extent to which I can influence or change the situation.

3. If I can influence or change the situation, I take the appropriate actions with the necessary intensity—but without getting overly attached to the end result.

4. If I can't change the situation, I remind myself that **while I don't know why this is occurring, I trust there is a good reason behind it, one that is for my benefit.** This allows me to more readily accept the "as is-ness" of the moment and thereby surrender to what's happening.

5. Finally, to leverage any learning, I ask myself, *"What is the gift that I need to uncover from this experience? What can I learn from it? How can I use it?"*

We can all benefit from solutions like "acceptance" and the technique described above for living with the stated paradox. They help us reduce the pain in our lives, and increase our joy.

WORDS *of* WISDOM

"In most cases, when you say, 'I,' it is the
ego speaking . . . It consists of thought and
emotion, a bundle of memories you identify
with as 'me and my story,' of habitual roles
you play without knowing it, of collective
identifications such as nationality, religion,
race, social class, or political allegiance."

ECKHART TOLLE
Author, *The Power of Now*

CHAPTER 11

Does Your EGO Get in Your Way?

WHAT IS EGO?

EGO could be an acronym for **E**veryone's **G**ot **O**ne. But what *is* it that everyone's got?

The *Oxford English Dictionary* defines ego as *"a person's sense of self-esteem or self-importance."* Ego is also Latin for "I."

Let me offer you a different definition ... Ego is that part of our personality or psyche that has a need or desire to:

- Feel a sense of significance or importance
- Judge people and events
- Let others know how special we are
- Feel superior to others
- Feel different from others
- Put our own needs before the needs of others
- Be right no matter what
- Control others
- Think, talk, and behave in terms of I, me, and mine

At its core, *ego is a feeling of **separateness***—that is, a separateness that exists between our:

1. Perceived self (or lower self) and our real self (or higher self), and
2. Our perceived self and others

This notion of separateness causes us to be, do, and live in a manner that creates:

- More pain than pleasure
- More conflict than harmony
- More disturbance than peace
- More sorrow than joy

HOW TO MANAGE YOUR EGO

Given that we all have an ego, what's the solution? While there isn't any easy quick fix, here are some helpful strategies for keeping the ego in check:

1. **Become aware.** Awareness is the prerequisite to any change. So the first step is to become conscious of your own behavior. Observe the motives behind how you think and what you do. For example, when you donate money, what is your primary motive—is it because you care deeply about helping others, or is it because it makes you feel less guilty? If it is the latter, you can be confident that it's the ego at work.

2. **Appreciate similarities.** Since at its core, ego is a feeling of separateness from others, a powerful strategy is to focus on noticing the similarities, as opposed to the differences, between people. Find deeper reasons why, at the most fundamental level, we are all the same. Explore ways to create a deeper connection with others who you perceive as being different from you.

3. **Don't take criticism personally.** When you get criticized, don't take it personally. When you take criticism personally, you know

it's the ego at work. Remember what others think of you is none of your business.

4. **Know your real self.** Get to know your real self—your higher self— the self that is the same for everyone and also the essence of who we are. Ask yourself: *"Who would I be if I were without my possessions, relationships, knowledge, job, etc.?"*

5. **Be present in the moment.** When you're worried about the past or the future, it's the ego at work. That's because it is very hard for the ego to exist when you're totally present in the moment.

6. **Resist comparisons.** Don't compare yourself with others. Don't compare what you have with what others have. Whenever you feel either superior or inferior in relation to someone, you can be sure that the ego is fully engaged in that moment.

7. **Do RAKs.** Do anonymous Random Acts of Kindness (RAKs) for others. When you take the focus off yourself, and instead focus on others, you reduce your ego. A small and fun action that I sometimes do is to pay the toll for the car behind me.

What steps do you want to take today to reduce your ego-oriented reactions and sense of separateness from the people in your life?

WORDS *of* WISDOM

"Your greatest gift lies beyond
the door named fear."

SUFI SAYING

CHAPTER 12

How Is FEAR Keeping You from Living Fully?

WHAT IS FEAR?

What does "fear" really mean? Here are a few definitions:

1. *An unpleasant emotion caused by the threat of danger, pain, or harm.* (*Oxford English Dictionary*)
2. FEAR = **F**alse **E**vidence **A**ppearing **R**eal
3. FEAR = **F**antasy **E**xperiences **A**ppearing **R**eal
4. FEAR = **F**orget **E**verything **A**nd **R**un!

WHAT IS THE SOURCE OF ALL FEAR?

Fear exists at two levels—the surface level and the source level:

1. **Surface** fear is the response you give when asked the question: *"What do you fear?"*
2. **Source** fear is the fear deep below the surface.

Confused? Here's an example: Let's say that you have a surface fear of speaking to large audiences, and you ask me to help you identify your source fear. To identify the source fear, I'll need to investigate this situation fully and ask you more questions like:

- *Why do you fear speaking to large audiences?*
- *What do you imagine when you think about public speaking?*
- *What is the worst thing you believe could happen?*
- *What would it mean to you if the worst thing did occur?*

Your answer to the above questions will most likely allow me to identify your source fear. And for 99% of the people who I have coached in overcoming the jitters with public speaking, the source fear is always the same: the fear associated with experiencing rejection from the audience.

While there are an infinite number of surface fears, our source fears—our deepest fears—can be grouped into three categories, as summarized below:

1. Fear of **loss**, either the loss of:
   - people, or
   - possessions

2. Fear of **pain**, either:
   - physical pain, or
   - psychological pain

3. Fear of **rejection**, from:
   - family, or
   - others

The diagram on the next page is a pictorial representation of the concepts discussed above.

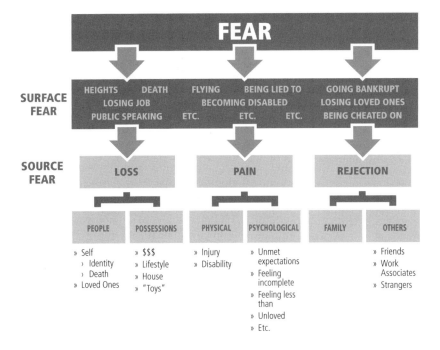

WHAT ARE THE CONSEQUENCES OF INDULGING FEAR?

Every emotion has its place, as does the emotion of fear—especially when it motivates us to take positive action. However, unnecessary indulgence in fear has some serious consequences, including:

- Feeling paralyzed and, as a result, never taking the actions required to pursue our goals and dreams
- Worrying about things that will most likely never happen
- Not enjoying the present moment
- Living our lives in a box—taking refuge from life inside our comfort zone
- Limiting the realization of our own potential

At the most serious levels, fear can cause rifts between nations. One of the driving emotions behind most wars and conflicts is the emotion of fear.

HOW TO DEAL WITH YOUR FEAR

Can we eliminate fear completely? Actually, eliminating fear is **not** a realistic goal for most of us, but we can learn how to deal with fear in a healthy manner.

Listed below are eight strategies that work:

1. **Acknowledge your fears.** In life, whatever you resist persists. The first step is to acknowledge what you fear. To get beyond the surface fear and discover the source fear, dig deeper and ask yourself questions like:
   - *What am I really frightened of?*
   - *What is the worst that could happen? What would that mean?*
   - *What do I believe that is causing me to be fearful?*

2. **Consider the likelihood.** Ask yourself: *"What is the probability of the thing I fear actually happening?"* In their book *Easy Peasey,* authors Allan and Barbara Pease point out what studies show about all the things we worry about in life:
   - 87% never happen.
   - 7% do happen.
   - 6% might happen, and you'll have some influence over the outcome.

   This means that most things in life that you worry about *won't* happen and that you have little to no control over the few things that *do* happen. So it just doesn't pay to worry about the things you fear.

3. **Be present.** Given that the object of fear can only manifest in the future, the biggest antidote to overcoming fear is to be present in the now. If you are totally present in the moment, you cannot experience the emotion of fear.

4. **Change your breathing.** The emotion of fear is accompanied by a specific breathing pattern. If you change your breathing pattern, you

can literally snap out of fear. Breathing in the following way can help you dissolve fear and become centered:

- Close your eyes.
- Bring your hands in toward your chest to "touch" your heart.
- Take 10 deep long breaths.
- With every breath, feel as if you are breathing into your heart.
- Continue the above process for as long as it takes you to feel centered and peaceful.

5. **Deploy your imagination constructively.** Often fear arises because we use our active imaginations to imagine the worst-case scenario. Active imagination can be a source of strength, but only if it's deployed resourcefully. Therefore, instead of visualizing worst-case scenarios, deploy your active imagination constructively. Visualize the best-case scenarios—the way you would like things to turn out.

6. **Manage your focus.** Change your focus from what you fear to something else that makes you happy. When you change focus, you change the way you feel.

7. **Get complete information.** Sometimes fear can be a result of inaccurate and/or incomplete information and/or inaccurate interpretation. Ask yourself:
   - *What information do I need?*
   - *What else could this situation mean?*

8. **Get moving.** To overcome any sense of immobility caused by fear, ask yourself: *"What steps can I take now to get moving?"*

This chapter is longer than most because fear can play such a big role in our lives, often an inhibiting one. A key point made is that much of what we fear never happens. After reading these pages and the included suggestions, how do you want to start changing the way you deal with your fears?

WORDS *of* WISDOM

"Thoughts are there because you think.
Thinking is not your nature. Your
nature is unalloyed happiness."

RAMANA MAHARISHI
(1879–1950)
Hindu Sage

CHAPTER 13

Do You Suffer from Compulsive Thinking?

COULD YOU ACTUALLY STOP THINKING?

What if I asked you to stop thinking for 24 hours? Could you do it? I suspect not. What about not thinking for even a few hours? Could you do that? Again, I suspect for the vast majority of us, the answer is "no."

Human beings typically have over 60,000 thoughts a day, with most of them being repetitive; by this, I mean that the thoughts we have today are the same thoughts we had yesterday as well as the day before yesterday! As a human race, we find it extremely difficult not to think—the majority of us are what I would call **compulsive thinkers engaged in compulsive thinking.** We haven't as yet found an **off** switch to our thinking.

At this stage, you may be wondering:

1. *Isn't thinking normal?*
2. *Am I a compulsive thinker?*
3. *What are the consequences of my compulsive thinking?*
4. *What can I do?*

Let's take each question in turn.

ISN'T THINKING NORMAL?

Thinking is obviously normal and has its place. As humans, our ability to think is our unique gift and strength, and our progress as a society is directly attributable to the quality of our individual and collective thinking. Problems arise when thinking becomes compulsive to such an extent that it becomes an addiction, and unfortunately this is an addiction that over 99.99% of humanity suffers from. Because a large proportion of the population suffers from this addiction, compulsive thinking is not seen as a problem and is therefore considered normal. But let's not confuse a majority opinion with what is in fact normal.

AM I A COMPULSIVE THINKER?

You are a compulsive thinker if one or more of the following conditions apply to you:

- Your mind never stops churning out thoughts.
- You can't be by yourself for extended periods, AND be quiet, AND be content, AND be peaceful.
- You believe to a large extent that "Because I think, therefore I am" as opposed to "Because I am, therefore I can think." In other words, you derive your sense of existence and identity from your ability to think.
- You believe that all solutions to your problems can only be addressed through thinking.

WHAT ARE THE CONSEQUENCES OF COMPULSIVE THINKING?

Just as any strength that is overused becomes a weakness, so it is with compulsive thinking. Some of the consequences and/or effects of compulsive thinking include:

- You are not present in your life. You're either in the past or the future, but hardly ever in the present moment. Being present in the now is the foundation for an outstanding quality of life.

- You are constantly chasing something or someone in order to feel happy. You're like a drug addict who will only be satisfied when they get the next high, and as with all drug addicts whose vicious cycle of chasing the next high never stops, so it is with you. What creates that "high" for you as a compulsive thinker might be different than what the drug addict seeks—for you, it's the next deal, the next million, the next relationship, the next job, the next term in public office, and so on, rather than a different and "better" drug—but the principle is the same.

- A deeper part of you continues to feel empty and exhausted in spite of what you have accomplished.

- You miss the big picture of experiencing because you use thinking to understand concepts that cannot be understood through thought.

The overriding consequence of compulsive thinking is that we end up becoming **"human doers"** as opposed to authentic **"human beings."** As such, compulsive thinking prevents us from fully experiencing life.

WHAT CAN YOU DO?

1. Recognize that thinking is a tool you have; it's not *who you are.* Who you are is so much more powerful than the thoughts you have, and even words are inadequate to describe your true essence.

2. Deploy your thinking faculties more consciously. In other words, consciously *choose* to think as opposed to suffering *involuntary* thought.

3. Don't take the negative thoughts you have personally (i.e., feel bad for having negative thoughts or associate your identity with them).

The mere act of taking negative thoughts personally, and then dwelling on those thoughts, is a major cause of personal unhappiness. The next time you find yourself taking the negative thoughts in your head personally, stop for a moment. Rather than judging these thoughts, just observe them. Don't get attached to the notion that *"I own these thoughts."* Pretend that these thoughts are like clouds in the sky, and as the clouds keep moving, let your thoughts move on in a similar fashion. When you detach your identity, your sense of self, from the thoughts in your head, you automatically experience more peace.

4. Shift your life balance more toward **being.** For most of us, the balance between doing and being is tilted more toward **doing.**

5. Respect and appreciate the present moment no matter what it is. The more you appreciate the now in whatever form it takes, the more you'll reduce the compulsive thinking process.

6. Regularly take time to be alone in quiet and peaceful surroundings. Learn to enjoy your own company. Let's face it—if you can't genuinely enjoy your own company, why would you expect others to?

Can you think of anything else you would add to this list?

A final note: Another downside to compulsive thinking is that not all of our thoughts are accurate. So *don't believe everything you think!* Inaccurate thinking can cause unnecessary unhappiness.

Bottom line: Life is more enjoyable when we allow ourselves to fully experience the present rather than being stuck in thoughts about the past or the future.

Words *of* Wisdom

"The thirst for objects is the greatest enemy of
peace. Desire causes distraction of various sorts . . .
The mind will be ever restless and hanker after the
objects. When this thirst dies, man enjoys peace."

SIVANANDA
(1887–1963)
Indian Spiritual Leader and
Founder of the Divine Light Society

CHAPTER 14

Do You Mistake These Three Deadly Enemies for Friends?

WARNING!

What I'm about to discuss here will most likely challenge some of your beliefs about life and success. It may even dispute traditional wisdom. The concepts could go against everything that has already made you successful and might even appear contradictory to what is covered in other parts of the book. You may experience a level of frustration, anger, and disappointment.

If you do relate to any of the above feelings, it's OK. I understand your reaction and I can also relate to it. All I ask is that you read this chapter and reflect on it with an open mind. If what I'm sharing does spark your curiosity, then I encourage you to explore it further. The essence of what I cover below forms the basis of gems contained in several Eastern philosophies, including Hinduism and Buddhism.

WHAT ARE THE THREE DEADLY ENEMIES?

The three deadly enemies disguised as friends are **desire, expectation, and attachment**.

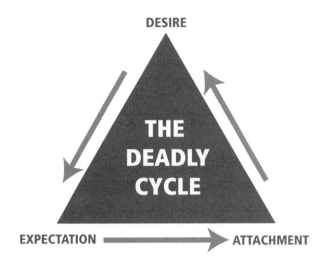

DESIRE

Desire is "the want for more" or "the want for something different," including to:

- Be like someone else
- Be somewhere else
- Be with someone else
- Do something else
- Feel something else
- Have something else
- Have more stuff (e.g., possessions, money)
- Live differently

EXPECTATION

Expectation is your fixed view about one or both of the following:

- *How* the desire should be realized (e.g., what specifically has to happen for you to feel that your desire has been fulfilled).

- *When* the desire should be fulfilled (e.g., the time frame within which you expect this to occur).

For example, if my desire is get a new job, my expectation could be that I will become CEO of IBM in the next six months.

ATTACHMENT

According to the *Encarta* English dictionary, attachment is: *"an emotional bond or tie to somebody or something."* Attachment to your desire is a feeling along the lines of: *"I must have what I desire, in the manner that I desire, and within the time frame I want."* In other words, attachment to all of the following three components:

- What you desire
- How the desire should be realized
- When your desire should be realized

According to Sri Sri Ravi Shankar, founder of the *Art of Living* organization and a Nobel Peace Prize nominee, *"Attachments cause feverish breath. Feverish breath takes away your peace of mind. And without peace of mind, you come apart and fall prey to misery."*

At this point, I can almost hear some of you asking: *"So what are you suggesting here, Rajeev, that I give up all my desires, expectations, and attachments?"*

Well, yes and no. If you believe you can give up all your desires, expectations, and attachments, that's great. But I believe that unless you have transcended to highly enlightened levels (e.g., sainthood), completely giving up desires would be a somewhat unattainable goal. According to the Vedas (the oldest Hindu sacred scriptures), the reason that we are reborn is that we still have *"vasanas"* (or unmet desires).

SO WHAT IS THE SOLUTION?

The answer lies across the following three dimensions:

1. Becoming more conscious of your desires, expectations, and attachments, and recognizing the extent to which these are controlling your life.

2. Moderating your desires, because desire is what starts off the vicious desire-expectation-attachment cycle.

3. Adjusting your desires, expectations, and attachments so that they are more aligned with your real spiritual self instead of your egoistic physical self. This adjustment involves redefining your desires, expectations, and attachments in the following manner:

DESIRE FOR	EXPECTATION THAT	ATTACHMENT TO
» Loving » Growing » Serving	» All events are there to help me and teach me. » No matter what happens, I can handle it. » The right people and resources will show up when I need them.	» Living in the present » Being authentic, and all that I can be » Embracing the paradox of life » Living my purpose

When you make these types of changes and adjustments, I believe you will experience more peace of mind in your life. So give it a try.

WORDS *of* WISDOM

"A man who has committed a mistake and doesn't correct it is committing another mistake."

CONFUCIUS
(551–479 B.C.)
Chinese Philosopher

CHAPTER 15

Are You Making Any of These Six Mistakes?

CICERO AND THE SIX MISTAKES

Marcus Tullius Cicero was a prominent Roman who lived 2,000 years ago. He was a statesman, poet, orator, and philosopher all combined into one. Cicero was an influential part of Roman history, and he was involved in many of the conflicts that involved historical characters such as Pompey, Caesar, and Brutus.

In one of his most famous treatises, Cicero outlined the six mistakes of man as he saw them evidenced in ancient Rome. Whilst these words were spoken 2,000 years ago, they are still as relevant for our times as they were for the heights of the Roman Empire so long ago. The six mistakes, as Cicero saw them, are:

1. The delusion that personal gain is made by crushing others.
2. The tendency to worry about things that cannot be changed or corrected.
3. Insisting that a thing is impossible because we can't accomplish it.
4. Refusing to set aside trivial differences.
5. Neglecting development and refinement of the mind, and not acquiring the habit of reading and study.
6. Attempting to compel others to believe and live as we do.

INTROSPECTION

The six mistakes, as outlined above, provide an excellent framework for some personal introspection. So I invite you to reflect on the profound wisdom of Cicero, and answer the following questions:

1. *To what extent are you making any of the six mistakes?*
2. *How are these mistakes restricting the quality of your life?*
3. *How committed are you to correcting any of your mistakes?*
4. *What are the few things that will make the biggest difference?*
5. *What would you do differently from now on?*

Isn't it incredible how this ancient wisdom continues to be relevant and valuable to us today?

WORDS *of* WISDOM

"Wisdom is knowing what to do next,
skill is knowing how to do it,
and virtue is doing it."

DAVID STARR JORDAN
(1851–1931)
Educator, Scientist, and Peace Activist

CHAPTER 16

What Are the Five Causes of Your Biggest Gap?

WHAT'S YOUR BIGGEST GAP?

In today's age, the lack of information or knowledge is not an issue. Thanks to advancements in technology, we are only a few clicks away from accessing knowledge about anything and everything. Rather, the biggest dilemma we face is to consistently act on the knowledge we already have.

I call this "the biggest gap" for most human beings—the gap between **knowing what to do** and **consistently doing what you know** or, in other words, "the Knowing-Doing Gap."

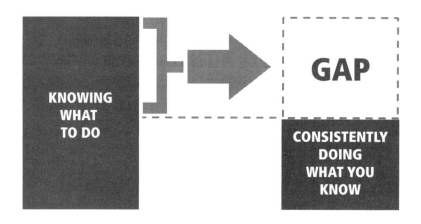

To what extent does the Knowing-Doing Gap apply to you? Let's look at some very basic, common examples:

- You know that exercise is good for you.
  But do you exercise regularly?
- You know that saving money is good for you.
  But do you save regularly?
- You know that meditation is good for you.
  But do you meditate regularly?

From your personal experience, what else can you add to the above? In which areas do you have a Knowing-Doing Gap?

In a minute, we'll take a look at the reasons that prevent us from closing the Knowing-Doing Gap. However, before proceeding further, I recommend that you select a specific area where you have a Knowing-Doing Gap that you want to close. By having a specific example in mind, you'll gain a more thorough understanding of the reasons why you haven't closed your gap, and also what will help you to progress.

WHAT PREVENTS YOU FROM CLOSING THE GAP?

The million-dollar question is *"What stops you from consistently acting on what you know?"*

There are five reasons:

1. **Not wanting it badly enough.** The precursor to all action is **desire.** If the desire to close the gap is not strong enough, then there are millions of excuses available to justify not taking action.

   Assess your situation. On a scale of 1 to 10 (1 = not at all, 10 = totally), how badly do you want to close the gap?

2. **Not willing to pay the price.** Even though the desire may be strong enough, if you're not willing to pay the price, then it's always easier

not to take the required actions. What is the price you may have to pay? It may include:

- Getting out of your comfort zone
- Changing your beliefs
- Forming new habits
- Learning new skills
- Investing time, money, and energy
- Delaying your need for instant gratification
- Overcoming fear

Assess your situation. On a scale of 1 to 10 (1 = not at all, 10 = totally), how willing are you to pay the price for closing the gap?

3. **Not taking the first step.** Some people want it badly enough and they're mentally willing to pay the price. However, they never take that first step. They never make a start. They get caught up in the *"I'll do it someday in the future"* scenario.

   Assess your situation. On a scale of 1 to 10 (1 = not at all, 10 = totally), to what extent have you taken the first step?

4. **Not taking the subsequent steps.** Some people want it badly enough, they're mentally willing to pay the price, and these folks even make a start. But they don't follow through the start with the subsequent steps. They either get distracted, become bored, or just lose the burning desire.

   Assess your situation. On a scale of 1 to 10 (1 = not at all, 10 = totally), to what extent have you followed your first steps with subsequent steps?

5. **Judging too soon.** Some people want it badly enough, they're mentally willing to pay the price, and they even take the first and subsequent steps. However, when they don't see results within the time frame and/or in the form they expect, they start to have doubts. They start to judge. The judgment is often in the form of questions such as: *"Is this worth it?"* or *"Am I doing the right thing?"* And often

this judgment causes people to reevaluate and rationalize, and very often give up, even though they may have been very close to experiencing all the rewards!

Assess your situation. On a scale of 1 to 10 (1 = not at all, 10 = totally), to what extent may you be judging too soon?

HOW TO CLOSE YOUR BIGGEST GAP

Now you know what's holding you back from closing the gap. So let's explore how you can make progress in this area.

1. **Develop a strong enough desire, a strong enough "why."**
   - Ask yourself, *"What would increase my desire to the point that having the gap is just not an option?"*
   - Once you've answered the above question, do whatever it takes to put into practice what you came up with.

2. **Be willing to pay the price.**
   - Identify the price you need to pay.
     ‣ *Who would you need to be?*
     ‣ *What would you need to do?*
     ‣ *How would you need to live?*
   - Pay the price.

3. **Take the first step.**
   - In the words of Greek philosopher Aristotle: *"The first step is what counts. First beginnings are hardest to make and as small and inconspicuous as they are potent in influence, but once they are made, it is easy to add to the rest."*
   - Identify the first few steps that you can take in the next 24 to 48 hours to make progress.
   - Take the first step.

4. **Take the subsequent steps.**
   - Being in motion is what creates momentum.
   - Do something every day, no matter how small, to maintain the momentum.

5. **Don't judge too soon.**
   - Be persistent.
   - Be patient—you may have to wait for the results. In the words of Norman Vincent Peale, the Father of Positive Thinking, *"It's always too soon to quit."*

After reading this chapter, you are more prepared than ever to use all your valuable knowledge. Closing "the Knowing-Doing Gap" may be just what you need to move forward in areas where you feel stuck.

WORDS *of* WISDOM

"I can teach anybody how to get what they want out of life. The problem is that I can't find anybody who can tell me what they want."

MARK TWAIN
(1834–1910)
Author, *The Adventures of Huckleberry Finn*

CHAPTER 17

Do You Have 100% Clarity?

WHY DO WE FAIL TO GET WHAT WE WANT?

The number-one reason people don't achieve what they want is because they don't clearly define what it is they want. Typically, when you ask someone what it is they want, one of the following three scenarios occurs:

1. They usually start by telling you what they don't want (examples: *"I don't want to be in my current role/job," "I don't want to have financial issues," "I don't want to be overweight,"* etc.).

2. They are not very specific. For example, they may say: *"I would like more money."* In my coaching sessions with clients, whenever I am given the *"I would like more money"* answer, I usually reach into my pocket, take out 20 cents, and say, *"Here you go, have 20 cents. Now you've achieved your outcome of having more money."* After the initial confusion and shock, clients usually get the message that they were not specific enough.

3. They go totally blank or give the *"I don't have the faintest idea"* kind of look, or they reply, *"I don't know."*

Without knowing precisely what it is that you want, you have no chance of being able to get it. It's impossible. At best, it will be hit and miss. Analogous to this is telling someone to go somewhere, but not telling them where it is that you want them to go. What are the odds that they will be able to get to the place that you have in mind?

WHAT DO WE NEED ABSOLUTE CLARITY ON?

To have any chance of achieving what you want, you must have absolute clarity on five key aspects. These key aspects, as illustrated below, are **Outcome, Reasons, Date, Evidence Procedure,** and **Current Position (ORDEC).**

1. **Outcome**
   - *What is my outcome?*
   - *What is it that I want?*
   - *What is the result that I'm trying to create?*

2. **Reasons**
   - *Why do I want to achieve my outcome?*
   - *What are the reasons that I'm pursuing this outcome?*

3. **Date**
   - *By what date do I want to achieve my outcome?*
   - *Why is this date important?*

4. **Evidence procedure**
   - *How will I know that I've achieved my outcome?*
   - *What will I see, hear, feel, or experience?*

5. **Current position**
   - *Where am I currently in relation to where I want to be?*

A SIMPLE EXAMPLE

To bring the ORDEC framework to life, I've outlined a simple example which you'll find below.

1. **Outcome**
   - To reach and maintain my ideal weight of 130 lbs.

2. **Reasons**
   - To feel even more healthy
   - To feel energetic

3. **Date**
   - I want to achieve my goal by June 30, 2009.

4. **Evidence procedure**
   - I step on the scales and the dial reads 130 lbs.

5. **Current position**
   - I currently weigh 165 lbs.

Can you see how being more clear about what you want will help you move forward? What goals do you need to think about more thoroughly?

WORDS *of* WISDOM

"The price of greatness is responsibility."

WINSTON CHURCHILL
(1874–1965)
Prime Minister of the United Kingdom

CHAPTER 18

Do You Take 100% Responsibility?

HOW RESPONSIBLE ARE YOU?

To what extent do you take responsibility for your life, including your current life situation? To what extent do you take responsibility when things don't go your way? What is your typical response when *bad* things happen to you or when your expectations are not met?

With over six billion people in the world today, blaming someone else for the way we feel is too easy. Blaming an event is also too easy. And while blaming someone else or the situation might seem to be our easiest option, and could even be justified at times, it's almost always the *wrong* option. This is because blame keeps you stuck in the Irresponsibility Trap and doesn't get you any closer to a resolution.

THE IRRESPONSIBILITY TRAP

As illustrated in the diagram on the next page, the "Irresponsibility Trap" is characterized by the following mindset:

1. You see the source or the cause of any perceived problem as being outside yourself.
   - *"It's not my fault."*

2. Because you see the problem as not being your fault, you don't feel you should and/or can do anything about addressing the problem.
   - *"Why should I do anything? I can't do much."*

3. You expect someone else to resolve the problem.
   - *"He/She/They should fix it."*

4. When nothing happens, or things don't happen as per your expectations, you feel betrayed.
   - *"It's not fair."*

THE INTELLIGENT CHOICE

Whatever the reality is, taking responsibility is always an intelligent choice because it helps you to move forward. However, taking responsibility doesn't mean becoming a martyr. Taking responsibility means that no matter what has caused the problem, you take responsibility for the following three things:

1. **Your part**
   - *What part of the problem do I own?*
   - *To what extent am I contributing to the problem?*

2. **How you feel about the problem**
   - Remind yourself: *"It's not the problem itself that's the issue; it's the meaning that I'm choosing to give this problem."*
   - *How can I give it a more empowering meaning?*

3. **Pursuing the required actions to resolve the situation**
   - *How can I be part of the solution?*
   - *What can I choose to do now to make progress in resolving the situation?*

Taking responsibility can reduce our anxiety as we free ourselves from the Irresponsibility Trap. We leave indecision and the related worry behind, and move by choice into positive action.

In what areas of your life could you be taking more responsibility?

WORDS *of* WISDOM

"The only way to discover the limits of the possible is to go beyond them into the impossible."

ARTHUR C. CLARKE
(1917–2008)
Author, *2001: A Space Odyssey*

CHAPTER 19

Is Your Comfort Zone Keeping You in Jail?

WHAT IS A COMFORT ZONE?

Are you familiar with the term "comfort zone"? Let me clarify, just in case you're not. Your comfort zone is like your very own *protective bubble*—a bubble within which you feel safe and comfortable. All of us have a comfort zone, and within this zone is everything that we are confident with, including:

- Situations
- Relationships
- Actions
- Knowledge
- Choices
- Decisions

Anytime you encounter anything within your comfort zone, you feel confident that you can handle it. That's because you have either dealt with the thing before, or with something at least somewhat similar. Conversely, whenever you come across something that is outside your comfort zone, you may experience a degree of uncertainty and even anxiety compared to what you experience when faced with things within it.

WHY IS IT IMPORTANT TO EXPAND
YOUR COMFORT ZONE?

To fully experience life, it is essential that we continue to grow. And growth requires you to have new experiences—whether that be working toward a PhD, climbing Mt. Everest, starting a new company, or taking on some other new role. And all new experiences occur in a realm outside your comfort zone.

If you're not willing to expand your comfort zone, you are, in effect, restricting your growth and, therefore, your fulfillment. Staying in your comfort zone could mean that you:

- Never realize your full potential
- Restrict your growth
- Don't achieve the rewards you desire or deserve
- Are left with unfulfilled dreams
- Live your life in a box
- Don't experience the freedom and fulfillment you seek
- Regress
- Die (emotionally, if not physically)!

In summary, therefore, the quality of your life is in direct proportion to the size of your comfort zone—the bigger your comfort zone, the better the quality of your life will be.

WHY DO WE RESIST EXPANDING OUR COMFORT ZONE?

Even though we intellectually know the benefits of expanding our comfort zone, we often resist it. Why is this? Well, when given the choice between the known and the unknown, most of us prefer the known. We are all creatures of comfort, and we crave security and certainty. Because we are, in a way, *addicted* to comfort, we oppose anything that may make us uncomfortable—even if it's for our own good. Since expanding our zone of comfort requires us to undertake NEW thoughts, decisions, and behaviors, we typically don't like it. We oppose change and resist getting outside the zone that feels familiar to us.

The irony is, however, that everything that's *within* your comfort zone now must have been, at some stage, *outside* your comfort zone.

HOW CAN WE EXPAND OUR COMFORT ZONE?

There's no limit to human potential, and what each one of us can be and do. Expanding your comfort zone, therefore, is not a one-off event. Instead, it's a lifelong iterative process composed of the following three steps:

1. **Get clear.**
   - *How is your comfort zone restricting you?*
   - *If you had no fear, who would you be, what would you do, and how would you live?*
   - *What's currently outside your comfort zone, which if you did it, would enrich your life even more?*
   - *What's something important that you've been avoiding because it makes you uncomfortable?*

2. **Get inspired.**
   - *What would inspire you to take action?*
   - Focus on the desired results, rather than what it would take to achieve them.

- Believe that the pleasure and pride you'll experience in going beyond what's comfortable will significantly outweigh any experience of discomfort.

3. **Get moving.**
   - Schedule the actions and just do it.
   - Get help if required (e.g., coach, mentor).
   - Celebrate the learning and the insights.

It can be important to *consciously* push ourselves beyond our comfort zone, because our "default setting" is to stay within it. How do you want to deliberately expand your comfort zone and move into higher levels of experience?

W O R D S *of* W I S D O M

"Incongruent individuals live lives that include
falseness and do not realize their potential.
They live lives that are not true to themselves,
to who they are on the inside."

C A R L R O G E R S
(1902–1987)
American Psychologist,
Father of Client-Centered Therapy

CHAPTER 20

How Congruent Are You?

WHAT IS CONGRUENCE?

Congruence is the powerful and positive feeling you experience when you hit the sweet spot of intersection between the following three ingredients:

1. What you are THINKING
2. What you are SAYING
3. What you are DOING

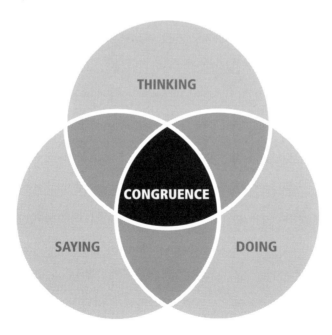

When you feel congruent, it's like being **in the zone.** Things flow *effortlessly.* You're in rhythm. You have momentum. You leap toward your goals. You radiate authenticity. Most of all, you feel *fulfilled.*

In contrast, anytime you feel incongruent, you experience internal conflict. You don't feel authentic. It feels like you're driving a car with the brakes on. There is drag and resistance. The journey is harder than it needs to be.

So, all in all, you get sub-optimal results when you're incongruent, and the overall journey is not very enjoyable either.

HOW TO BECOME MORE CONGRUENT

The feeling of congruence is situational and not absolute. This means that in certain situations we may feel very congruent, while in others we may not be that way as much. Therefore the first step in getting to congruence is to identify the specific situations where you may be experiencing incongruence. Once you've identified a particular situation, go through the following process to make progress:

1. Write down your answers to the following questions:
   - *What are you thinking?*
   - *What are you saying?*
   - *What are you doing?*

2. Review your answers to the above questions to discover the elements that are not in congruence.

3. Identify the root causes of your incongruence. Ask yourself: *"What's behind the incongruence that I'm experiencing? What's really going on?"* Listed below are some potential causes of incongruence:

   - **A conflict between the head and the heart**
     "My heart tells me to start my own business, but my head tells me to stay in my current job."

- **Fear**

  "I'm a bit scared of leaving my job. What if my business doesn't work out?"

- **Conflict of beliefs**

  "I know that having my own business is the right thing to do BUT I don't believe that I can be successful."

- **Habits not aligned to what is required**

  "To be successful in my business, I need to be able to sell. But I don't really want to learn how to sell."

- **Conflict of values**

  "I want my own business AND I don't want to take any risks."

- **Conflict of priorities**

  "Should I start my new business now or should I focus on a steady and predictable income?"

4. Identify and execute the few actions that would make the biggest difference in addressing the root causes.

Being in congruence is like having all of your "selves" (your Thinking Self, Saying Self, and Doing Self) on the same team playing to win the same game. You won't be in conflict with yourself, and therefore can do your best in any situation.

WORDS *of* WISDOM

"Some of the biggest challenges in relationships
come from the fact that most people enter
a relationship in order to get something:
they're trying to find someone who's going
to make them feel good. In reality, the only
way a relationship will last is if you see your
relationship as a place that you go to give,
and not a place that you go to take."

ANTHONY ROBBINS
Best-Selling Author, Peak Performance Coach

CHAPTER 21

How Fulfilling Is Your Intimate Relationship?

RELATIONSHIPS = GOOD NEWS + BAD NEWS

When it comes to intimate relationships, there's both good news and bad news.

The good news is that these relationships can be the source of infinite joy, happiness, and fulfillment. When we're deeply in love with another person, the joy we experience is indescribable. Time stops. There is no better feeling.

The bad news is that issues in intimate relationships can also be the source of the deepest pain we experience. When things aren't going well in this area, nothing else seems to matter. We feel hurt, angry, and sad. We feel alone. We can't focus on anything else. To numb the pain, we try to distract ourselves by whatever means possible.

CONFLICTS IN INTIMATE RELATIONSHIPS

So what causes issues in intimate relationships? Here are the top 15 reasons:

1. **You don't understand each other.** Just as oxygen is crucial to physical survival, *being understood* is essential to emotional survival. When your partner doesn't feel understood, it's almost as if they are

being deprived of oxygen. They feel suffocated. And feeling suffocated is not conducive to a happy relationship.

2. **You put your needs first.** When you consistently put your own needs and interests before those of your partner, you make them feel like a second-class citizen. And not surprisingly, no one likes to feel that way. Over time, this builds up resentment and causes a high degree of conflict.

3. **You both have a different "love language."** Gary Chapman, in his best-selling book, *The Five Love Languages,* suggests that we all have a primary language that allows us to feel the most love. These love languages include:
   - Physical touch
   - Quality time
   - Acts of service
   - Words of affirmation
   - Gifts

   Issues in relationships occur when our primary love language is different from our partner's, and we express love in *our* primary love language rather than in their preferred way. For example, to make my wife feel more loved, I give her gifts. However, in reality, she would feel more deeply loved if I spent additional quality time with her, as opposed to presenting her with gifts.

   To overcome the love language issues, you need to:

   - Be aware of your partner's primary love language(s), and
   - Express love to your partner in their language, and not your own.

4. **You don't feel respected and/or trusted.** The values of respect and trust are the foundation of any long-term relationship. When these foundations are not in place, the whole relationship is built on shaky ground and subject to consistent tremors and fluctuations.

5. **You cannot be yourself.** When you feel you can't be yourself and have to instead be something else in order to be accepted, you feel fake and inauthentic. This breeds deep unhappiness and eats you up inside like an emotional cancer.

6. **You have vastly different value systems.** For a long-term relationship to be sustainable, there needs to be some degree of alignment around values. For example, if you place a high value on family and children and your partner is totally the opposite, then it is more than likely that you will experience conflict.

7. **You don't communicate in a manner that allows you to resolve issues.** It's natural that any two people will experience issues or problems at some stage in their relationship. What's important is *how you communicate* with each other when faced with problems. Are you able to talk in a way that allows you to get to the root of the issue, resolve it, and go forward? Or do you get stuck for long periods of time when you don't see eye to eye?

8. **You consistently put your dreams and goals before the relationship.** If your partner often feels that your dreams and goals are more important than they are, they will begin to believe that there will always be something more important to you than them. They'll think that they could never be the most important priority in your life. And this generates resentment because, on some level, your partner will feel rejection.

9. **You don't say, "I'm sorry."** Making mistakes is part of being human. However, the biggest mistake is not saying "sorry" when you know you're the one who's in the wrong.

10. **You are sexually incompatible.** You have pronounced differences in your sexual needs:
    - What you like and don't like is different from what your partner likes and doesn't like.

- What is acceptable and unacceptable to you is different from what your partner finds acceptable and not acceptable.
- The frequency of your desire for sex is different from your partner's.

11. **Your partner doesn't make you feel special.** After the basic need to be understood, the next major psychological human requirement is to feel appreciated. Conflicts in intimate relationships often arise because one partner doesn't make the other feel appreciated, wanted, or special.

12. **You are not "in love" with your partner.** You may get along with your partner, be comfortable with him/her, or even be best friends. Still, if you're not "in love" with your partner, this will cause conflict at some point.

13. **You are constantly criticizing your partner.** A common cancer in relationships is constant criticism. This happens when you are more focused on what's missing or what's wrong than on what's already there or what's great. Criticism often builds up over time, and before you know it, it can take over and destroy the entire relationship.

14. **You are consistently "not present" in the relationship.** I'm talking here about either physical or emotional absence, or both. Though a common cliché claims that "absence makes the heart grow fonder," I believe consistent absence makes the attachment become weaker and the relationship sour.

15. **You don't forgive.** As discussed above, it's natural that you and your partner will make mistakes over the course of your relationship. That's part of being human. However, when you can't forgive your partner's mistakes, you'll tend to withhold your love. And when you withhold your love, it will result in pain—for both of you. The principle *"To err is human, to forgive divine"* is at its truest when it refers to intimate relationships.

Does your closest intimate relationship have some of the conflicts discussed above? Which conflicts seem most important to address? What initial steps could you take to help heal these conflicts?

RE-IMAGINE YOUR PHILOSOPHY

- What are the vital few philosophies that make the biggest difference?
- To what extent are you living in alignment with these philosophies?
- How do you embed more empowering philosophies into your daily life?

WORDS *of* WISDOM

"That deep emotional conviction
of the presence of a superior reasoning power,
which is revealed in the incomprehensible universe,
forms my idea of God."

ALBERT EINSTEIN
(1879–1955)
American (German-born) Physicist

CHAPTER 22

A Higher Intelligence
Is at Play

IS THERE *MORE* TO LIFE?

- *Is there more to life than what we perceive through our five senses?*
- *Is there more than what we experience consciously?*
- *Is there a broader universal intelligence?*

I believe the answer to all the above questions is YES. There is infinitely more than what we can see and experience consciously. This *more* is something that is larger than us—something larger than life itself. It is the universal force of creation—the infinite intelligence.

There are many other *labels* that you may use to describe this infinite intelligence:

- God, by whatever name
- Divine intelligence
- Higher power
- Universal intelligence
- Supreme intelligence
- Grand Organized Design
- Great Organized Designer
- The Source
- Infinite power

- Ultimate awareness
- Infinite field of unfolding possibilities
- Organizing intelligence
- Atman

Do you have any other names for this higher power?

TAPPING INTO THE UNIVERSAL INTELLIGENCE

What you call this universal intelligence is secondary to my purpose here. What is important is the extent to which you can tap into this intelligence for your benefit—and for the benefit of others. And your success in accessing this all-powerful intelligence is dependant on the following two factors:

1. **The extent to which you *believe* in this intelligence.** The stronger your trust or belief in a higher intelligence, the more likely that you'll be able to leverage this intelligence.

2. **The extent to which you can *tune* in to this intelligence.** Tuning in to this powerful intelligence is somewhat like tuning in to your favorite radio station. Once you've tuned in to a radio station, the news, conversations, and music flow effortlessly and beautifully. So it is with tuning in to this higher power. Once you've tuned in to this power, you're directly connected with the source that can fulfill all your dreams and aspirations, and help you resolve even the toughest of issues.

But how does one tune in to this powerful intelligence? This is somewhat of a personal question. I don't believe there is a right way or a wrong way. There are **numerous ways.**

On a personal level, I have found the following practices to be useful for tuning in to the universal intelligence:

- Prayer
- Meditation
- Spending time in nature
- Being silent
- Writing down my thoughts, feelings, issues, and desires
- Asking for help from the universal intelligence
- Showing appreciation
- Showing gratitude
- Helping others

How about you? Based on your experience, what has worked for you for tuning in to the universal intelligence? What else could you add to methods I've listed above?

The key point to note is this: No matter what technique or strategy you use, there are two fundamental principles related to tuning in to the universal intelligence. These principles, as illustrated below, are the principles of **expectancy** and **openness.** When we expect guidance from a higher power and look for it, we are more likely to receive it.

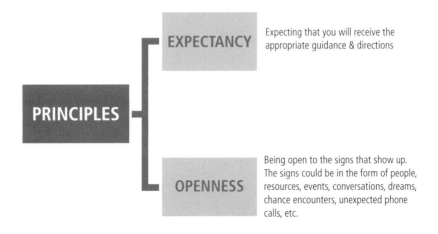

EXPECTANCY — Expecting that you will receive the appropriate guidance & directions

PRINCIPLES

OPENNESS — Being open to the signs that show up. The signs could be in the form of people, resources, events, conversations, dreams, chance encounters, unexpected phone calls, etc.

In closing, consider this quote:

"To trust in the force that moves the universe is faith.
Faith isn't blind, it's visionary.
Faith is believing that the universe is on our side,
and that the universe knows what it's doing."

AUTHOR UNKNOWN

WORDS *of* WISDOM

"Wisdom is looking back at your life and realizing
that every single event, person, place, and idea
was part of the perfected experience you needed
to build your dream. Not one was a mistake."

DR. JOHN F. DEMARTINI
Author and Founder of the Concourse of Wisdom
School of Philosophy and Healing

CHAPTER 23

Most Events Are Blessings in Disguise

HAVE YOU EVER MISJUDGED A NOTABLE INCIDENT?

Have you ever had an event in your life which you initially judged as painful, but then you came to view it in a more positive light over time?

Maybe losing your job caused you to start your own successful business. Or maybe leaving a dysfunctional relationship allowed you to attract your soul mate. Or perhaps it was your first heart attack that prompted you to change your eating habits and work toward better health. Maybe you can't relate to any of these examples, but you can think of others that are more specific to you.

I know I've had numerous such events. And each time, I've come to realize (in hindsight) the futility of judging the event too soon. I believe that every event in my life, no matter how painful, has served me on my life's path.

WHAT CAUSES US TO MISJUDGE?

What causes us to judge an event as painful at first, even though we may look back at it in a more positive light later? It is our rampant tendency to judge too quickly, a habit that you and I have had plenty of practice with! We are *constantly* judging. And what do we judge? Everything from other people, events, and experiences, to even ourselves. Typically, anything that creates pleasure for us, we judge as "good," and anything that creates pain for us, we view as "bad."

Looking at events (and experiences and people) in this manner is a fundamental cause of our misery. By categorizing events as bad, we trigger within ourselves a chain reaction of negative emotions—feelings such as sadness, anger, despair, and hopelessness. These emotions suck up our energy and leave us feeling drained.

A BETTER APPROACH

Is there a better way? Yes, and here's what I suggest:

1. **Pause.** Whenever you find yourself judging an event (or an experience, or a person) as bad, stop for a moment. By stopping to pause, you create some space between the trigger and your response. And by creating this space, you increase the chances that you will *consciously choose* what the event means, as opposed to automatically jumping to conclusions.

2. **Explore.** Once you have created a space, use that opportunity to explore what else the event could mean. To do this, ask yourself the following four questions:
   - *Can I really be sure that this event is bad?*
   - *How can I be so sure that this event is not for my benefit?*
   - *What else could this event mean?*
   - *Is there any possibility that over time I could look back at this event in a more positive light?*

By considering the above questions, at the very least, you create some doubt about your automatic negative response. And in doing so, you create an opening to consider other possibilities.

Helen Keller, an American author, activist and lecturer, and the first deafblind person to graduate from college, once commented: *"When one door of happiness closes, another opens; but often we look so long at the closed door that we do not see the one which has been opened for us."*

To look for the empowering meaning within any event, I highly recommend a belief along the lines of:

"I don't know why this event is affecting me and/or what it really means. While at this stage it seems painful and/or unjust, I can't fully understand the bigger picture yet and how this event may serve me over time. I trust that with time the disguised benefits in this challenge will eventually reveal themselves, and I will be able to fully appreciate how this seemingly 'bad' situation has served me positively."

A fantastic book (and now a movie) that captures the essence of what's covered in this chapter is Mitch Albom's *The Five People You Meet in Heaven*. Read the book or watch the movie to be inspired about acting on what you've just read. You'll also gain insight into how people misjudge events and even underestimate the value that their own life has to others.

WORDS *of* WISDOM

"Everything you need you already have. You
are complete right now, you are a whole,
total person, not an apprentice person on the
way to someplace else. Your completeness
must be understood by you and experienced
in your thoughts as your own reality."

BEVERLY SILLS
(1929–2007)
American Opera Singer

CHAPTER 24

Remember that You Are Already Complete

WHAT DO BABIES HAVE THAT ADULTS DON'T?

Have you ever observed a typical baby when it's three months old, six months old, or even a year old? Let's assume you have. Now if I were to ask you to describe the baby's *nature*, what would you say?

My guess is that most people would use some of the following words: *peaceful, joyful, present, playful, loving, innocent, blissful, expressive, content, happy.* Would you agree that there is a feeling of completeness in a baby?

Now let's imagine a typical adult. How would you describe a typical adult's *nature*? To what extent would you use the same words that you used to describe a baby's nature? To what extent would you say that there's a feeling of completeness in a typical adult?

The biggest difference between a typical baby's nature and an adult's, I believe, is in **the extent of the sense of completeness** that a baby feels versus what an adult experiences. While a baby has an innate sense of completeness, a typical adult rarely feels complete on a consistent basis.

WHAT HAPPENS IN THE TRANSITION?

Somewhere along the developmental path from baby to adult, this sense of completeness is lost. And for most of humanity that triggers the ultimate search—a search that for most people lasts a lifetime and perhaps even beyond! And the outcome we're really seeking from this search is to regain that total sense of completeness—to feel a sense of total worthiness about ourselves.

To regain this sense of completeness, most of us use many different strategies. We pursue all sorts of interests, relationships, careers, businesses, adventures, spiritual paths, and so on in an effort to have this feeling.

But no matter how much success we experience in our endeavors, none of our pursuits seem to give us a sustainable feeling of completeness.

HOW TO REGAIN AND SUSTAIN THE COMPLETENESS

So what should we do? How do we get to feel this sense of completeness, this feeling of **being enough,** on a sustainable basis?

1. First, realize that no matter what your life situation is (what you do or don't do, or what you have or don't have), **you are already complete**—this is your true nature, your very essence.

2. Second, remember that **"no-thing"** (read nothing) will ever make you *feel* complete. While things may momentarily give you a sense of pleasure, things can't provide the sustainable feeling of total completeness.

3. Finally, remember that in order to experience your innate sense of completeness, you only need to **clear away the blockages** that may be getting in your way. One such blockage is a set of rules about **what has to happen before you can feel complete.** For example, you may have a rule that you can only feel totally worthy and complete if you have no negative thoughts at all at any time. What are the odds of that happening? *Not much*—at least if you're human!

Perhaps the biggest irony is that the moment we behave as if we're complete, not only do we experience peace and happiness, but we also attract the material success that we desire! So why not start recognizing your completeness more often, beginning today? It is your natural state, the way you were created and intended.

WORDS *of* WISDOM

"It is good to have an end to journey toward;
but it is the journey that matters, in the end."

URSULA LE GUIN
Science Fiction Writer

Life Is 99% Journey,
1% Destination

WHERE DO YOU SPEND THE MOST TIME?

What's the most elite sporting event in the world? The Olympic games, of course.

It's an event that occurs every four years, where the very best athletes in the world compete for the ultimate prize—*a gold medal*. One of the most celebrated events in the Olympics is the 100-meter race—a race to determine the fastest man and woman in the world. This race is typically over in less than 10 seconds for men and less than 12 seconds for women.

How long do you think the athletes spend preparing for the 100-meter race that ends in less than 12 seconds? My guess is at least four years, if not longer. So, more than 99% of their time is spent **preparing** for the Olympics—or, in other words, in the journey.

You may be thinking, *"Yes, but that's the Olympics and I'm not an athlete. So what has that got to do with me?"* Well, think about any goal that you've ever achieved in your life. And as you think about this goal, answer the following questions:

1. *How long did you spend preparing and taking action to achieve your specific goal, i.e., in the journey?*

2. *How long did you spend either participating in the actual event and/ or celebrating once you had achieved the goal, i.e., at the destination?*

3. *How long did that celebratory feeling last before you started to wonder, "What else?" or "What next?" or "Is that it?"*

HOW DO YOU TYPICALLY TREAT THE JOURNEY?

Between journey and destination, most people focus on the destination only. They worry and obsess about whether or not they will achieve their goal. And when it comes to the journey, they view it only as a means to an end. And because of this attitude, they never really end up enjoying the journey. What a huge waste that is!

What I'm getting at is that no matter what your specific situation is, you spend the vast proportion of your time in the "journey" phase. Keeping the end in mind is obviously important. However, equally important—if not *more* important—is to make the most of your journey, since most of your time is spent there.

HOW TO MAXIMIZE FULFILLMENT IN THE JOURNEY

The magic formula for making the most of your journey is as follows:

1. **Be fully present at all times.** Don't waste the present moment by either regretting the past or worrying about the future. Instead, just be present in the moment.

2. **Appreciate whatever shows up in your journey.** Sometimes the obstacles and detours on the journey are essential lessons that we need to learn to maximize our talents and potential.

3. **Be detached from the destination as much as possible.** Instead, focus on giving your best effort here and now to the task at hand.

4. **Celebrate progress.** Take moments along the journey to pause and feel gratitude and pride for all the progress that you've already made on your journey. Focus on how far you've come, as opposed to how much farther you may have to go.

Now remember some of the "journeys" that you've been on in your life, including the one you recalled earlier in this chapter. Then think of all that you got out of being on the path to those goals. Now use the power of the magic formula above to get the most out of the journey you're on today.

W O R D S *of* W I S D O M

"The reality of life and the underlying universal
laws are usually formed from a paradox—
which means 'both/and' rather than 'either/or.'
To be on the path of your life purpose is to
learn to be comfortable with paradox."

C A R O L   A D R I E N N E
Author, *The Purpose of Your Life*

CHAPTER 26

Life Is a Paradox

CONFUSING CHOICES ARE A PART OF LIFE

We live in a world in which things often appear to be inconsistent, even paradoxical. We are often faced with choices that seem to be in conflict. Such choices include:

- *Do I cling to certainty or step into the unknown?*
- *Do I live in the now or plan for the future?*
- *Do I go for instant gratification or delay my gratification?*
- *Do I fight or do I surrender?*

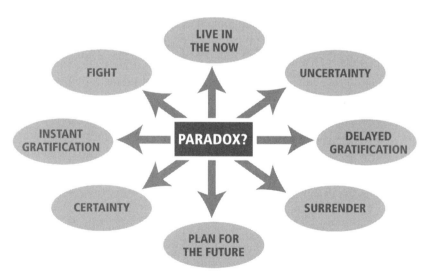

LEARNING TO NAVIGATE LIFE'S CONTRADICTIONS

Finding answers to such questions is not easy. The answers are generally far from obvious, and choosing between them can feel a lot like trying to choose between two rights. So what do we do? I recommend keeping the following three principles in mind:

1. Recognize the paradoxical nature of the world we live in.
2. Accept the paradox that we live in—*"That's just the way it is."*
3. Resolve the paradox on a case-by-case basis. Where the paradox does appear to be a stumbling block, the key is to get a clear vision of your desired outcome. The clearer you are on your outcome, the easier it will be to know what to do.

Since life is a dance between seeming contradictions, the key is to:

> *Dance elegantly in the paradoxical mystery of life.*

W O R D S *of* W I S D O M

"Mathematics, rightly viewed, possesses not
only truth, but supreme beauty—a beauty
cold and austere, like that of sculpture."

B E R T R A N D   R U S S E L L
(1872–1970)
Philosopher and Mathematician,
Nobel Laureate in Literature

CHAPTER 27

The Mathematics of Life

A NEW WAY OF LOOKING AT LIFE PRINCIPLES

Mathematics is a very precise subject. But life, unlike mathematics, is not that precise. Life is more like a dance between the sciences and the arts.

But what if life could be expressed just as precisely as mathematics? If that were so, what might be some of the **foundational life formulas** that would be taught to every student of life?

These are my top 10 foundational life formulas:

Formula	Meaning
1. Behavior = motive + mood + thinking patterns	Your behavior at any point in time is a function of your motives or your intent AND your mood or your emotional state at that instant AND your habitual thinking patterns.
2. Freedom = know yourself + be yourself	True freedom comes from knowing yourself at a deep level and having the courage to express yourself authentically.
3. Wealth = peace + contentment + happiness	True wealth is not measured by your bank balance. Rather, true wealth is the extent of the peace, contentment, and happiness you feel on a consistent basis.

Formula	Meaning
4. Self-esteem = self-acceptance + self-love	Your self-esteem to a large degree depends on the extent to which you accept and love yourself.
5. Success = vision + personal psychology + execution	Success in any venture is a function of your vision, your personal psychology (e.g., beliefs, attitudes), and your ability to act on your vision.
6. Peace = presence + gratitude	The peace you experience at any moment is determined by the extent to which you are present in the moment and the extent of gratitude you feel in that moment.
7. Feeling = focus + meaning	What you feel at any moment is a function of what you're focusing on and the meaning you attach to whatever it is that you're focused on.
8. Wisdom = knowledge + action	To know something and not to act on it is not wisdom. Wisdom is when you put into action what you know.
9. Natural essence = love + joy + playfulness + compassion + peace	Our natural essence—i.e., what is deep inside all of us—is an abundance of love, joy, playfulness, compassion, and peace.
10. You - your ego - your fears = universal creative source	When you operate without ego and without fears, you tap into the universal source of creation.

Which of the 10 formulas calls to you more than the others? To keep it front of mind, copy the life formula onto a Post-It® or index card and place it where you'll see it often throughout the day. Soon you'll incorporate the formula into your way of thinking. Then come back and do the same thing again with another formula, repeating this process as many times as you find helpful.

WORDS *of* WISDOM

"Life can be found only in the present moment.
The past is gone, the future is not yet here, and
if we do not go back to ourselves in the present
moment, we cannot be in touch with life."

THICH NHAT HANH
Zen Master

CHAPTER 28

Make Love to the Present Moment

WHAT HAPPENS WHEN YOU MAKE LOVE?

This is a rather personal question, I know. But I do have a serious point. Other than the obvious pleasure you feel, when you make love, is it not true that you're absolutely *in the moment*? I seriously hope that you're not thinking about what you did during the day or what you've got planned for tomorrow, but instead are totally present *in that wonderful moment*.

Well, what if you made love to the present moment? What would happen if more of your moments were blessed with the same level of presence that you have when making love? If that were the case, how much more alive would you feel? How much more content could you be? How much more fulfillment could you experience?

Being present in the moment is a powerful force. All life happens in the present moment, and when you are not present, you miss the experience of life.

WHAT STOPS US FROM BEING PRESENT?

The biggest obstacle to the present moment is the **egoistic mind.** This aspect of our mind thrives on thinking about the past or the future. As such, it never really allows us to be in the present. The irony is that the past and the future don't really exist; life happens always in the present. *What do I mean by that?* I mean that when the past happened, it happened in the NOW, and when the future happens, it will also happen in the NOW. As such, the only moment that ever exists is the present moment.

HOW TO BECOME MORE PRESENT

There are many strategies for fully embracing the NOW. Listed below are six ways to enhance your level of presence.

1. **Notice when you're not present.** If you notice yourself not being present, bring your attention to the NOW; in the process, you'll automatically become present in that moment. The following quote from best-selling author and peak performance coach Anthony Robbins sums it up best: *"When you notice it's not working, it's working."*

2. **Accept the present moment.** When you unconditionally accept whatever it is that you're feeling and experiencing in the moment, you automatically embrace the moment.

3. **Eliminate worry.** If you're not present, it's because you're either worrying about the past (which can't be changed) or worrying about the future (which only exists in your imagination). I am by no means suggesting that you shouldn't plan for the future. Instead, what I'm proposing is that when you do plan, you do so consciously and deliberately, and with total presence.

4. **Set up supportive practices.** Do practices that expand your level of presence. Meditation is one such practice. Through meditation, you are able to train your mind to be still and present in the moment.

5. **Establish a ritual to bring you back to the present moment.** When I become aware that I'm not present, I clap my hands and say out loud: *"Attention—here and now."* This forces me out of my thinking mind (which is either thinking about the past or imagining the

future) and into the present moment. What can you do that will literally snap you into the present moment anytime you notice yourself not being present?

6. **Practice *being present*.** Generally speaking, women are better at being present and also noticing when someone isn't present. So any men wanting to train themselves to be more present could practice the following exercise with a trusted female partner.

- Sit across from your partner and look into her eyes without saying a word. Ask your partner to tap you on the knee whenever she notices that you're not being present with her.
- Listen to your partner's conversation with "total presence." Again, ask her to give you feedback whenever she notices that you're not present.

In addition, one of the best books that I've read on the subject of being present is Eckhart Tolle's *The Power of Now.* If you'd like further support for staying in the present moment, I urge you to pick up a copy of it. Tolle's clear explanations will provide further insights as you develop the skill of being in the present, which becomes strengthened with practice.

WORDS *of* WISDOM

"The present is never our goal: the past and
present are our means: the future alone is
our goal. Thus, we never live but we hope
to live; and always hoping to be happy, it
is inevitable that we will never be so."

BLAISE PASCAL
(1623–1662)
French Mathematician and Philosopher

CHAPTER 29

"And" Your Life

HOW MOST PEOPLE LIVE

Most of us live our lives within the paradigm of: *"If A, then B."* What does this mean? Let me share some examples of this:

- If I make more money, then I can feel successful.
- If I get that promotion, then I can feel good.
- If I can lose weight, then I can feel beautiful.
- If I can fall in love, then I can feel happy.

The common pattern is along the lines of: *"**If** I achieve what I want, **then** I can feel the feeling I want to feel."*

The point is this: We live our lives **conditionally.** We make our feelings contingent on the achievement of a goal or a desire. And by doing that, we don't give ourselves the permission to feel good **right now.** Living in this way creates more stress and anxiety than is necessary.

A SMARTER WAY TO LIVE

I believe there is a better way to live. A smarter alternative to conditional living is to **"and"** your life. In case you're wondering what **"anding"** your life actually means, let me explain by revisiting the above examples. When you **"and"** your life, your thinking changes in the following manner:

FROM (Conditional living)	TO (And living)
If I make more money, **then** I can feel successful.	I feel successful **and** I intend to make more money.
If I get that promotion, **then** I can feel good.	I feel good **and** I intend to get that promotion.
If I can lose weight, **then** I can feel beautiful.	I feel beautiful **and** I intend to lose weight.
If I can fall in love, **then** I can feel happy.	I feel happy **and** I intend to fall in love.

Your revised thought pattern is along the lines of: *"I feel the feeling I want to feel **and** I intend to achieve what I want."* Let me stress that this is no mere matter of semantics. When you **"and"** your life, you think differently, you feel differently, and you act differently.

Why is **"anding"** your life a better approach? There are two key reasons:

1. You get to experience your desired feelings **immediately.**

2. When you experience your desired feelings, you get into an **empowered** state of being. And from this empowered state, you're more likely to do what is necessary to achieve your goal. You'll also enjoy the journey more along the way.

The diagram on the next page sums up the concepts discussed above.

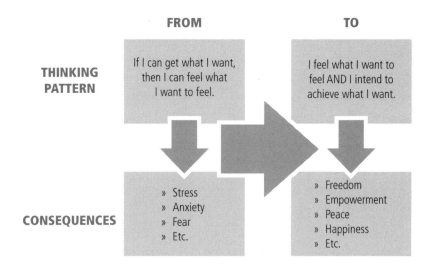

I think you may be surprised at the powerful impact that "anding" your life can make. Due to the new perspective that comes with this approach, we are much more effective in the world. Also, because we're tapping into our optimal feelings, we feel happier, more satisfied, and have more fun. In what specific ways do you think applying the "anding" philosophy could make a difference in your life?

WORDS *of* WISDOM

"What a man thinks of himself, that is what
determines, or rather indicates, his fate."

HENRY DAVID THOREAU
(1817–1862)
Philosopher, Author, Naturalist

CHAPTER 30

Don't Confuse Net Worth with Self-Worth

SELF-WORTH AND NET WORTH

Are you familiar with the words "self-worth" and "net worth"? What do these words mean to you? Do you believe there is a relationship between them?

Sometimes we confuse our net worth with our self-worth. We believe our self-worth is a function of our net worth, and so when our net worth does not meet our expectations, we don't feel good about ourselves. We feel inadequate. We feel as if we are **less than** and **not enough**.

Confusing your net worth with your self-worth is a fundamental error in judgment, and one that can result in a lower quality of life than you desire and/or deserve.

GETTING IT RIGHT

1. Remember that your self-worth is not the same as your net worth. Your self-worth is:
   - How you feel about yourself
   - Your self-concept
   - Your self-image
   - Your level of self-esteem
   - The extent to which you accept yourself

- The level of respect you have for yourself
- The value you place on yourself

Your net worth is:
- A number
- A financial amount that can be expressed in any currency
- The difference between the financial value of all you own LESS what you owe

No matter what your net worth is, it is your birthright to have a high sense of self-worth.

2. Even though your net worth doesn't determine your self-worth, there is, however, a link between your self-worth and net worth. A higher self-worth can result in a higher net worth. Let me explain why. When you have a high self-worth, here is what happens:
- You feel comfortable within your own skin.
- You place a higher value on yourself.
- You are not driven by the need to please others.
- You stand tall and act with confidence.
- You don't hesitate to let your light shine.

All in all, you embody a posture for success—you become a magnet for attracting the appropriate resources and opportunities. You take the necessary actions, not because it will increase your self-worth, but because you know it is the right thing to do.

The diagram on the next page accurately depicts the relationship between self-worth and net worth.

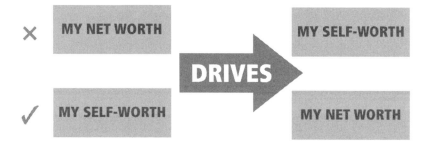

3. To enhance your self-worth even more, ask yourself the following key questions:
   - *On a scale of 1 to 10 (1 = no self-worth, 10 = very high self-worth), what is my current level of self-worth?*
   - *What would change if I started operating from a higher degree of self-worth?*
   - *What is holding me back from having a higher self-worth?*
   - *What will cause me to have a higher self-worth than I currently have?*
   - *What do I need to believe in order to accept myself, respect myself, and love myself even more?*
   - *What will I do differently from now on? When will I start?*

Once you've answered the above questions, reflect on your answers, and most importantly, take action on what you've discovered.

WORDS *of* WISDOM

"Wealth is the product of man's capacity to think."

AYN RAND
(1905–1982)
Author, *The Fountainhead*
and *Atlas Shrugged*

CHAPTER 31

You Are Already a Millionaire!

ARE YOU A MILLIONAIRE?

Do you think that you're a millionaire? If you answered "no," let me attempt to convince you that you are indeed already a millionaire. So, if you will, please answer the following few questions:

1. *Would you sell your heart for a $1 million? How about $10 million?*
2. *Would you sell your legs for $1 million?*
3. *Would you sell your arms for $1 million?*
4. *Would you sell your brain for $1 million?*
5. *Would you sell your children for $1 million?*

My guess is that you answered "no" to most, if not all, of these questions. If you're a parent, selling the kids for $1 million might be tempting sometimes. But seriously, the point I'm making is that you already have **assets** that are worth several million dollars. In effect, that makes you a millionaire!

Applying the above analogy to your life, the key point is this: We almost always have more resources than we realize. At the same time, we often blame the lack of resources for our failure to realize our dreams and goals. But the real reason, other than the absence of desire, is often a lack of *resourcefulness* and not the lack of resources.

HOW TO MAKE THE MOST OF WHAT YOU'VE GOT

To make the most of what you've got, regularly ask yourself the following questions:

1. *What are some of the resources that I already have that I may have overlooked?*

    Some of these resources may include:
    - Your unique background
    - The skills you have
    - Your diverse experiences
    - The people you know and the people that they know
    - Your energy, passion, and determination
    - Time
    - Money
    - Access to insights from experts

2. *What would happen if I deployed all of my resources to their fullest extent?*

3. *How can I become even more resourceful?*

When we take stock of the true extent of all our resources, we feel more powerful and put ourselves in the position to be fully supported. So make it a habit to ask yourself the three questions above from time to time, especially during periods when you feel your resources are lacking.

W O R D S *of* W I S D O M

"Our greatest power is the power of choice;
our greatest freedom lies in the
exercise of our power of choice."

G E O R G E   W I L L I A M   C U R T I S
(1824–1892)
American Writer and Public Speaker

CHAPTER 32

Claim Your Greatest Gift

CHOICES

CHOICE is our most under-exercised birthright. But what is "choice"? The *Oxford English Dictionary* defines choice as:

- The right or ability to choose
- The act of choosing between possibilities

Here's how most people view choices:

1. Most people believe that in some instances they have choices and in other instances they don't.

2. Typically, people don't feel that they have a choice when they find themselves in one or more of the following situations:
   - They feel forced to make decisions.
   - They don't like any of the options that they have to choose from.

3. When people feel that they don't have a choice, they feel trapped and helpless.

4. Feeling trapped and helpless confirms their belief that *"I don't have a choice."*

5. Consistently living with the belief that *"I don't have a choice"* breeds a victim mentality.

6. Living with a victim mentality lowers the quality of people's lives. It even attracts more situations which reinforce the illusion that *"I don't have a choice."*

FUNDAMENTAL TRUTHS ABOUT CHOICES

No matter what the absolute truth is, the extent to which you own your life will depend on your beliefs about choices. Here is what I believe about choices:

1. We all have choices.

2. All choices have consequences.

3. We can exercise our choices, but we can't necessarily control the consequences of our choices.

4. The more choices we believe we have, the more resources we have at our disposal.

5. The wisdom we exercise in our choices determines the quality of our lives and the fulfillment we experience.

6. The eight fundamental choices that influence our lives are summarized in the diagram on the next page. These choices translate to the acronym: "BE FAME TO."

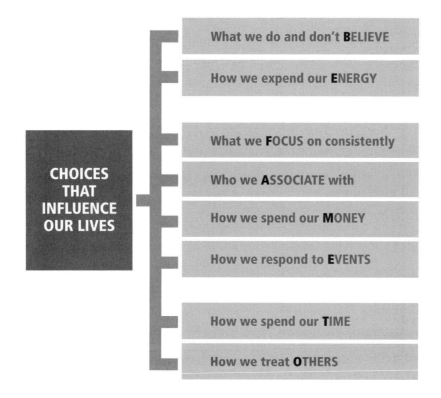

WHAT IS YOUR PERSPECTIVE ON CHOICES?

To become aware of how you view choices, please answer the following questions:

1. *What are your beliefs about choices?*
2. *How have your beliefs about choices influenced the quality of your life?*
3. *How have the major choices you've made shaped your life?*
4. *In what areas do you believe that you don't have a choice?*
5. *For items you identified in point 4, what would happen if you did start to believe in and exercise your choices?*

6. *What are some new choices that you can make **right now**, choices that you know will take your life to the next level?*

To become further inspired to recognize and act on your power of choice, consider the following quote from U.S. Senator Robert F. Bennett:

> *"If you can control the process of choosing, you can take control of all aspects of your life. You can find the freedom that comes from being in charge of yourself."*

Words *of* Wisdom

"The only conquests which are permanent and leave no regrets are our conquests over ourselves."

Napoleon Bonaparte
(1769–1821)
Emperor of the French

CHAPTER 33

Your Most Profitable Investment

WHICH IS THE BETTER INVESTMENT?

Some people are quite happy to spend $2,000 on a holiday. However, these same folks would think 10 times before spending $1,000 on a training course that had the potential, for example, to improve their communication skills or even their marriage. And while many people would be fine with paying $100 per hour for a personal trainer to keep their bodies in shape, they might be reluctant to buy a $30 book to enhance their emotional intelligence. Why?

The reason is this . . . when it comes to choosing between instant pleasure and delayed gratification, we go for the instant pleasure far more often. To clarify what I mean, let's review this concept in the context of the above example. It's easy to see that while the returns from a holiday are instant (e.g., suntan, relaxation, fun), the returns from a training course are typically delayed. It may take a while before you notice the benefits. Not only that, more effort is involved in attending the course and then putting into practice what you've learned.

WHY INVEST IN YOURSELF?

A fundamental law of life is that all living creatures either grow or die. There is no in-between—we are either growing or we are regressing.

Investing in yourself is not only **the best investment** you can make, it's also the best form of insurance against becoming obsolete, especially in your professional field. For example, doctors, these days, have to undergo a minimum level of ongoing training just to be able to continue to practice.

Investing in yourself ensures your continual growth, and the returns from this investment are multifold—you have the potential to improve **all areas** of your life as a result of this investment. For example, when you improve your communication and influencing skills, not only do you improve your productivity at work, but you also enhance your intimate relationships and your parenting skills.

OPTIONS FOR INVESTING IN YOURSELF

There are several options available to help you maximize your personal and professional development. These resources include:

1. **Books, CDs, DVDs.** It amazes me how many people don't read books. Yet for often less than $50, you can get access to thinking from experts in virtually any field. As an example, if you were to read one book a week, in 10 years you would have read 520 books and in 20 years more than 1,000 books. This would be enough to put you in the top 1% of experts in any field.

2. **Coaching.** All elite athletes have professional coaches. These coaches are not necessarily the best players in the sport, but are the best at maximizing the potential of the athlete. Why, then, do so few people have coaches to help guide them through the ultimate sport—the sport of life?

3. **Seminars, conferences, retreats.** You can attend multi-day events where you can totally immerse yourself in learning from some of the best teachers in their field.

4. **Formal study.** You can complete university courses at many different levels (e.g., certificate, diploma, undergraduate, postgraduate).

Over the last 15 years, I have personally invested over $200,000 in my personal and professional development. I consider this to be my best investment yet because who I have become and the results I have achieved, both tangible and intangible, are priceless.

What about you? What can you do to invest in yourself? What could you do that will enhance your personal and professional effectiveness and fulfillment? I invite you to come up with an **"Investment in Myself Plan (IMP),"** and to make a commitment to execute your plan.

WORDS *of* WISDOM

"Ask and you shall receive. Seek and you will
find; knock and it will be opened to you."

MATTHEW 7:7

CHAPTER 34

Ask and You Shall Receive

CAN YOU ACCELERATE WHAT YOU WANT?

A big part of our lives is spent striving for more. We set and achieve goals throughout our lives. To help us accomplish our goals, there are extensive resources at hand—including books, CDs, DVDs, specialist seminars, and numerous experts. Even though most of what I've read, listened to, or attended in person has been of tremendous value, I have often wondered if there was a way to accelerate the manifestation process.

In my search for answers, I found some clues in the Bible, in the form of the following statement: *"Ask and you shall receive."*

According to the "Good Book," the fastest way to get what you want is to ask for what you want. So the key questions are:

1. *Who do you ask?*
2. *How do you ask?*
3. *Why does the process work?*

WHO DO YOU ASK?

You ask the universe. You ask the source. You ask the universal intelligence—an intelligence that's hard to see and difficult to explain with words, but nevertheless makes everything possible. That is, if you choose to believe it.

HOW DO YOU ASK?

To fast-track what you want, I recommend the following simple, but powerful, four-step process:

1. **Specify.** Be very specific about what you want.

2. **Ask.** To ask for what you want, do the following actions:
   - Visualize the desired outcome or the results—remember, what you visualize, you materialize.
   - Write down your goal as if it has already come true (e.g., *"I am so happy and grateful that I have achieved my goal of <insert your goal>"*).
   - Keep your written goals where you can see them every day, e.g., in your wallet, in several places in your home (e.g., bathroom, study), in your office.
   - Share your goals with people who are supportive, encouraging, and/or could help.
   - Read your goals every day to enforce your intention to your subconscious and the universe.

3. **Act.** Do your bit by taking the necessary actions. At the same time, don't get overly attached to the desired outcome.

4. **Thank.** Give thanks, no matter what experiences and/or interim results show up along the way. Realize that there are no coincidences, and that everything is part of the bigger plan—the **Grand Organized Design.** Therefore, accept the unfolding of the Grand Organized Design.

WHY DOES THIS PROCESS WORK?

Although I don't know for sure why this process works, I do, however, have a hypothesis. And my hypothesis is that the process works for the following two reasons:

1. **You tap into the universal law of attraction.** By asking for what you want, you engage the help of a universal intelligence. And this universal intelligence is so much greater than the collective human wisdom. The net result is that, as you take a single step toward your goal, the universe takes 100,000 steps to help you.

2. **You activate your Reticular Activating System (RAS).** Your RAS, located at the base of your brain, is like a programmed missile designed to find its target. When you decide what you want, the RAS is activated and it starts looking for opportunities. Opportunities in the form of:
   - People who could help you
   - Information that may be useful
   - Resources that you need

To engage the full power of your RAS, the key is to be very specific. That's because the more specific you are about what you want, the more powerfully the RAS can do its job!

Now think about what you specifically want to ask for. Does it have to do with your work life, intimate relationship, or is it more about something you want personally for yourself? Once you've identified a goal, use the four steps described above in the section "How Do You Ask?" as a process for doing your asking.

W O R D S *of* W I S D O M

"A human being experiences himself, his thoughts
and feelings, as something separated from the rest,
a kind of optical delusion from his consciousness.
This delusion is a kind of prison for us, restricting
us to our personal desires and to affection for
a few persons nearest to us. Our task must be
to free ourselves from this prison by widening
our circle of compassion to embrace all living
creatures and the whole of nature in its beauty."

ALBERT EINSTEIN
(1879–1955)
American (German-born) Physicist

CHAPTER 35

Expand Your CQ

WHAT IS CQ?

You may have heard of "IQ" (Intelligence Quotient), "EQ" (Emotional Quotient), and maybe even "SQ" (Spiritual Quotient). But you may be wondering, *"What exactly is a CQ?"*

CQ stands for your **Caring Quotient**—a measure of the breadth and depth of your caring.

Your **breadth of caring** means **what and/or who you care about.** For example, if you had to pick from the following list, what would you choose?

- Self
- Family
- Community
- Country
- World
- Universe

Your **depth of caring,** on the other hand, is a measure of **how much** you care. For instance if you picked self, family, and community in the above example, the next question is this: *"Do you care about yourself, your family, and your community at the same level?"* Your answer to this question indicates your **depth** of caring.

WHY EXPAND YOUR CQ?

Caring is both a selfish and an unselfish act—unselfish because you get to help others, and selfish because the more you help others, the more rewards you enjoy. Rewards in the form of the:

- Growth you realize
- Fulfillment you feel
- Peace, joy, and contentment you experience

Personally, I have found the above to be very true. Let me share what I mean. Several years ago, I made a decision to raise $50,000 to help the less privileged. At the time I made the decision, I had no idea how I was going to make this happen. But immediately after I decided, things fell into place almost magically—the right people showed up to join me and the right resources became available. We had great momentum, and along the journey, each of us experienced tremendous personal growth and fulfillment—in addition to helping others. The charity, *Making a Difference (MaD),* is now into its seventh year and we have raised over $100,000 for several local and international causes.

On a more global level, let me share a quick story about Tiger Woods. Tiger Woods has already established himself as arguably the greatest golfer in history, but he hopes his legacy will focus instead on his contribution to society. He created the Tiger Woods Foundation with his father, Earl, in 1996, focusing on kids and providing them with an opportunity to learn life skills.

Tiger Woods recently made this comment: *"Golf is something that I do selfishly for myself. I have a competitive side and that's how I express it. But as far as my tombstone is concerned, hopefully it will read something more of what I am trying to do for kids. That would be so much more ultimate than winning any golf tournament. The joy I get from winning a major championship doesn't even compare to the feeling I get when a kid writes a letter saying: 'Thank you so much. You have changed my life.' That, to me, is what it's all about."*

So all in all, I hope you are even more convinced that caring is not only good for others, but good for you, too. And also that no matter what your situation may be, there is an opportunity to extend your breadth and depth of caring. When in doubt, I remember the words of American President Theodore Roosevelt, who wisely said: *"Nobody cares how much you know until they know how much you care."*

HOW TO EXPAND YOUR CARING

For this work, I suggest following a four-step process:

1. **Determine your current CQ.** To improve anything, you must first know your starting position. Therefore, the first step in expanding your CQ is to determine your current CQ. To do so, go through the following process:

   a. **Determine your breadth of caring.** Answer the following question: *"Who do you care about?"* You may use the following categories as a starting point: Self, Family, Community, Country, World, Universe. Feel free to customize this list as necessary.

   b. **Determine your depth of caring.** For each item in your above list, answer the following question: *"On a scale of 1 to 10 (1 = not at all, 10 = a lot), how much do you care?"*

   c. **Fill in your answers in a table,** such as below:

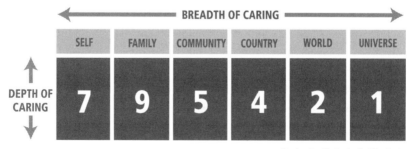

		BREADTH OF CARING			
SELF	FAMILY	COMMUNITY	COUNTRY	WORLD	UNIVERSE
7	9	5	4	2	1

DEPTH OF CARING

Scale: 1 = Not at all, 10 = Lots

2. **Identify what to focus on.** Review your own version of the table on the previous page. Decide what areas you want to focus on and why.

3. **Create a plan.** In generating ideas about your plan for broadening and deepening your caring, ask yourself:
   - *What are the few things that could make the biggest difference?*
   - *Who could I be?*
   - *What could I do?*
   - *How could I live?*

   Think outside the box or, in other words, think *creatively*. Caring can come in many different forms—whether that be listening to someone who really needs you to listen deeply, empathizing with others, doing random acts of kindness, playing your part in preserving the environment, and so on.

4. **Execute your plan.** The final step in the process is to schedule and execute the specific elements of your plan.

Today we are seeing more and more high-profile individuals getting involved in causes. Though some may also be motivated by the related publicity value, it is encouraging to see so many working to make a difference. Now, with the help of the processes in this chapter, you, too, are in a position to increase your level of caring.

WORDS *of* WISDOM

"Treat someone like you expect the best,
and pretty soon they'll behave like that."

ANONYMOUS

CHAPTER 36

Become a 90% Person

THE CHOICE

All of us have gifts, strengths, and talents—things we are great at. Equally, all of us have weaknesses—areas where we can improve. Given these realities, there are a couple of questions to consider:

1. *What do we focus on more, i.e., expanding our strengths or rectifying our weaknesses?*
2. *What do we do with our weaknesses?*

There are two popular points of view regarding strengths and weaknesses:

1. One point of view advocates that you focus most of your energy to address your weaknesses.
2. Another view recommends that you direct most of your energy to enhancing your strengths.

I belong to the latter camp, and therefore recommend that you focus 90% of your energy on cultivating your gifts and your unique talents. I term this as "becoming a 90% person."

WHY BECOME A 90% PERSON?

There are three benefits to becoming a 90% person:

1. **It's good for you.** When you play to your strengths, not only do you feel more fulfilled, but you also achieve outstanding results.

2. **It's good for others.** When you become a 90% person, you tend to observe and acknowledge other people's strengths, rather than focus on their weaknesses. By doing that, you help to ignite the potential of others.

3. **It's good for the team.** When everyone in the team plays to their strengths, you get a very engaged and high-performing team.

WHAT ABOUT ADDRESSING WEAKNESSES?

So what are you meant to do with your weaknesses? Do you just ignore them? No, I'm not suggesting that. What I'm suggesting is that you focus 90% of your energy on your talents and find other ways to work around your shortcomings. As a strategy for addressing your weaknesses, I suggest the following process:

1. **Identify** the extent to which your weaknesses are preventing you from expressing your true magnificence.

2. **Prioritize** the areas you most want to improve—what improvements would make the biggest difference to your quality of life?

3. **Implement** a strategy to spend no more than 10% of your energy and time on addressing the weaknesses you identified in point 2 above.

4. **Partner** with others who could compensate for the areas that you're weak in.

By focusing most of your energy on your gifts, strengths, and talents while still addressing your weaknesses in this way, you'll become more aware of your abilities and be more effective. As a 90% person, you'll be offering the world and yourself the opportunity to experience the best of what you're all about.

WORDS *of* WISDOM

"The teacher who is indeed wise does not bid
you to enter the house of his wisdom but rather
leads you to the threshold of your mind."

KAHLIL GIBRAN
(1883–1931)
Lebanese-American Poet

CHAPTER 37

Help Anyone Anytime
With Anything

YOU DON'T NEED TO KNOW THE ANSWERS

Most of us are born helpers, meaning it's in our nature to try to help other people. Yet even though our intentions may be sound, at times we do not feel capable of helping. This is because we don't have all the answers. Meanwhile, we believe that in order to help someone, we must have the correct answers so that we can advise appropriately. Advising can, of course, be very useful in the appropriate context. However, there are also other ways that you can be of assistance.

An additional item to have in your "help tool kit" is what I call the **Coach Approach** to helping others. In this approach, you don't need to know the answers. Instead, you create a relationship that allows the person you're helping to uncover the answers for themselves.

Carl Rogers, one of the preeminent psychologists of the 20th century, has shared the following insights about how he changed his approach to helping clients: *"In the early professional years, I was asking the question: 'How can I treat or cure or change this person?' Now I would phrase the question in this way: 'How can I provide a relationship which this person may use for his own personal growth?' "*

There are two advantages of the Coach Approach to helping others:

1. **Greater ownership.** When people come up with the answers themselves, they have stronger ownership of the solutions. Therefore they are more likely to follow through on the necessary actions.

2. **Increased flexibility.** The Coach Approach is a more flexible approach than advising. That's because it works in both types of situations:

   - First, the ones where you *do* think you know the answers and,
   - Secondly, also in those times when you *don't* believe that you have the answers.

As such, the Coach Approach can allow you to help anyone, anytime, with anything.

IMPLEMENTING THE COACH APPROACH

To put the Coach Approach into practice, one of the key abilities you need is the ability to ask the right questions. Constructing the right questions is both an art and a science. However, any question that helps someone make progress is a great question. In my experience, I have found the following set of questions to be effective in a variety of situations:

To understand the desired outcome

1. *What is it that you want?*
2. *What is the problem you want to address?*
3. *What is the outcome you desire from this situation?*

To gauge the level of commitment

1. *Why is achieving your outcome important to you?*
2. *How important is it for you to address and resolve your situation?*
3. *On a scale of 1 to 10 (1 = not at all, 10 = completely), how committed are you to achieving your outcome? If not a 10, what would it take for you to be a 10?*

To clarify obstacles (real or perceived)

1. *What has prevented you to date from achieving your outcome?*
2. *What is preventing you from achieving your outcome right now?*
3. *What do you believe are the real obstacles to making progress?*

To develop a Making Progress Plan (MPP)

1. *What is one thing you can do that will make the biggest difference right now?*
2. *If you had already achieved your outcome, what would you have done?*
3. *What actions are you committed to taking?*
4. *When will you take these actions?*
5. *What support do you need, and from whom?*

While encouraging the person to make a plan, focus them toward the solutions that feel the most plausible and achievable. You can then offer further help by agreeing on a time to get back together to review progress.

WORDS *of* WISDOM

"This is no time for ease and comfort.
It is the time to dare and endure."

WINSTON CHURCHILL
(1874–1965)
Prime Minister of the United Kingdom

CHAPTER 38

Choose Serving Over Pleasing

WHEN "WHAT'S RIGHT" CONFLICTS WITH PLEASING

Sometimes in life, we face difficult choices—choices between doing what's pleasurable and doing what's right. This is because the option of doing what's right *and* pleasurable at the same time is not always viable.

This is often true in the context of parenting; there are numerous situations where parents have to decide between **pleasing** their children versus **serving** their children. As you think about this, you may be wondering:

1. *What's the difference between pleasing and serving?*
2. *How do I make the right choice?*

"Pleasing," in the context of parenting, is *doing whatever it takes to make your child **happy in the moment**, regardless of whether what you do is the right thing for your child or not.*

"Serving," on the other hand, is ***doing what's in the best interests of your child**, even though it may not feel pleasant in the moment and/or may make your child unhappy or cranky right now.*

TAKING THE HIGHER ROAD

OK, let's say you're facing a situation where you can't both please and serve your child. What do you do?

In my experience, taking the pleasing option is almost always the *easier* option. However, in the long run, taking the pleasing option is almost *never the right option.* I know whenever I have made the harder decision to serve rather than please, I've always looked back and felt proud of my choice.

In case you are not a parent and therefore think this concept doesn't apply to you, think again. Even though I've used parenting as an example, the choice between serving and pleasing exists across many contexts—including relationships, business, finances, and so on.

A CAVEAT

I'll add one caveat to all of the above, and that is this: The recommended "serving" approach assumes that you know what's best for someone else. That can seem presumptuous, and maybe even arrogant. This is not the intent of what I'm suggesting. Thus I recommend that you apply the philosophy above selectively and after careful due diligence, and only in situations where there is absolutely no doubt as to what would be in the best interests of someone else. This philosophy is about serving from a place of no ego, and with the absolute purest of intentions.

WORDS *of* WISDOM

"Change is not made without inconvenience,
even from worse to better."

R ICHARD H OOKER
(c.1554–1600)
English Clergyman and Theologian

CHAPTER 39

The Three Levers for Changing Any Habit

WOULD YOU LIKE TO CHANGE ANY HABITS?

Are there any behaviors that you would rather not indulge in? Are there any habits that you want to change?

Assuming that you, like most people, have habits and/or behaviors that you want to change, the key question is this: *What's stopping you from successfully making the desired changes?*

As you think about your answer, check to see if any of your reasons include the following:

1. *I don't know how to change.*
2. *I've tried in the past and it hasn't worked.*
3. *I'm trying but it's not working.*
4. *It takes time to change.*
5. *I will change when it's more convenient.*

WHY HAVEN'T YOU CHANGED?

While the above reasons may appear rational and justified on the surface, deep down you probably know that these are not the real reasons. This is because changing any habit or behavior is much more a function of **your desire,** as opposed to a function of knowing how to change or the time it takes to change. The main reason you haven't changed is because you haven't reached the "tipping point for change," i.e., the point where changing the desired habit or behavior is an absolute priority.

HOW TO REACH THE TIPPING POINT FOR CHANGE

There are three main Levers you can use to reach your tipping point for change. As shown in the diagram below, these Levers are: **Pain, Gain, and Inspiration.**

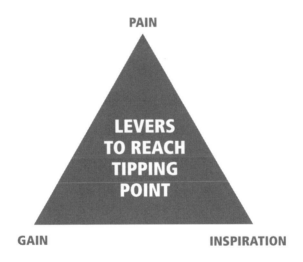

Although these Levers can be used in isolation of each other, the real power is when you:

a. Apply *all* the Levers, and
b. You feel the impact of the Levers emotionally.

Let's briefly look at each of the Levers in turn.

1. **The Pain Lever.** To apply this Lever, you need to reach the point where you feel that the **ongoing pain of continuing** with the existing

habit is so much greater than **the pain you link with changing** the habit. To get to this point, deliberately ask yourself a set of pain-inducing questions such as:

- *How is this habit or behavior constraining my life?*
- *What have I failed to be or do because of this habit or behavior?*
- *What would it mean if I don't change this habit or behavior now?*

2. **The Gain Lever.** To apply this Lever, you need to reach the point where you feel that **the gain you'll experience** in overcoming the limiting habit or behavior is greater than the **comfortable feeling of putting up with the habit.** To get to this point, deliberately ask yourself a set of gain-inducing questions such as:

- *What else can I be and do if I overcome this limiting habit or behavior?*
- *How different will my life be in 5, 10, or 15 years without this limiting habit or behavior?*
- *If I conquered this habit or behavior, what else can I overcome that I didn't think was possible?*

3. **The Inspiration Lever.** To apply this Lever, you need to reach a point where you are totally inspired to change. When you're totally inspired by a cause, you feel a burning desire inside you and you're determined to succeed, no matter what the obstacles may be. You know deep within your soul that unless you change your habit or behavior, you won't be successful and fulfilled. To get to the point of inspiration-driven change, ask yourself powerful questions such as:

- *What is my passionate cause? What do I aspire to be and do? How do I want to live?*
- *How is my habit or behavior restricting me in fully realizing my passionate cause?*
- *Why must I change this habit or behavior now?*

Note: In thinking about the three Levers, be aware that there can be another inhibiting factor when we feel stuck in a habit or behavior and it is related to Lever 1 (The Pain Lever). This is fear—the negative things you're afraid might happen if you start to do things differently. Take a moment to think about whether you have any fears related to changing. If so, are they realistic? What can you do to prevent any projected negative outcomes from happening?

After switching your focus with the help of the three Levers, plus working through any fears related to changing, you can be free to start ridding yourself of the undesired habit or behavior pattern. I also encourage you to get hold of Anthony Robbins' *Awaken the Giant Within*—it is an outstanding book about overcoming disempowering habits and creating lasting change.

WORDS *of* WISDOM

"What we do for us dies with us. What we do for
others and the world remains and is immortal."

A LBERT P INE
(d. 1851)
English Author

CHAPTER 40

Become an Instrument of Peace

INSPIRATION FROM ONE OF THE MOST BELOVED SAINTS

Assisi is a small village in Italy. In the 13th century, a soldier, the son of a rich merchant, lived there. Propelled by a vision to serve God, he gave up his material life to spend the remainder of his days living by and spreading the message of Christ. He later came to be known as Saint Francis of Assisi. The city of San Francisco is named after him. The following excerpt from his teaching is a great illustration of how to be an instrument of peace.

LORD, LET ME BE AN INSTRUMENT OF THY PEACE

Where there is hatred, let me sow love;
Where there is injury, pardon;
Where there is doubt, faith;
Where there is despair, light;
Where there is sadness, joy;
O, divine Master, grant that I may not so much seek
To be consoled as to console;
To be understood as to understand;
To be loved as to love;
For it is in the giving that we receive;

It is in pardoning that we are pardoned;
It is in dying to self that we are born to eternal life.

As you reflect on the above words, what do you feel? What does the above prayer mean to you? I invite you to consider ways that you too can become an instrument of peace in the world.

OPTIMIZE YOUR PRACTICES

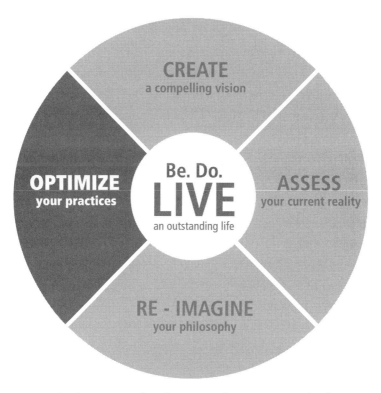

- Recognize to what degree you're practicing the few things that make the biggest difference.
- Act on the vital few practices that make the biggest difference.
- Embed new practices to further enhance your quality of life.

W O R D S *of* W I S D O M

"Did you ever see an unhappy horse?
Did you ever see a bird that had the blues?
One reason why birds and horses are not unhappy
is because they are not trying to impress
other birds and horses."

D A L E   C A R N E G I E
(1888–1955)
Author, *How to Win Friends and Influence People*

CHAPTER 41

Be Authentic

HOW UNIQUE ARE YOU?

Even though at one level we are all the same, at another level we are all unique. How unique? Despite the fact that there are over six billion people in the world, no two people have the same DNA (unless they are identical twins). And like our physical DNA, we also have a non-physical DNA—something that defines our authentic self, our real self.

One reason that so many people are unhappy is because they're not being their authentic selves. They pretend to be something they're not. They try to be like someone else.

There are two main explanations for why most people are not fully authentic:

1. **They don't know their authentic selves.** Most of us don't really know ourselves at a deeper level, i.e., who we are at an authentic level. We become so accustomed to the masks we wear that we mistake our masks for our real authentic selves.

2. **They want validation from others.** We often feel pressured by other people's expectations of us. Then, at some level, we believe that we're more likely to be accepted, respected, and/or loved if we perform in the expected way.

HOW TO BE MORE AUTHENTIC

Before discussing how to be more authentic, let's quickly review what being authentic *is not*. Being authentic *doesn't* mean behaving like a jerk, not improving yourself, or hiding behind excuses like: *"That's just the way I am . . . take it or leave it!"*

Instead, being A-U-T-H-E-N-T-I-C means:

1. **A**ccepting who you are.

   All of us have multiple personalities. Some personalities we are proud of, and some personalities we'd rather not acknowledge, even to ourselves.

   Monica Furlong, in her book, *Genuine Fake: a Biography of Alan Watts*, quotes Watts (best known as an interpreter of Eastern philosophies, including Zen Buddhism) as saying: *"It has often been said that the human being is a combination of angel and animal, a spirit imprisoned in flesh, a descent of divinity into materiality, charged with the duty of transforming the gross elements of the lower world into the image of God . . . Not to cherish both the angel and the animal, both the spirit and the flesh, is to renounce the whole interest and greatness of being human."*

   A fundamental step in authentic living is therefore to first acknowledge ALL of yourself—the good, the bad, and even the ugly!

2. **U**nderstanding your true nature.

   What is your real nature? What has been a constant aspect of your personality throughout your life? Who would you be if you were completely authentic? What are your unique gifts and talents? What is your uniqueness? What makes you light up like a Christmas tree? By answering the above questions, you'll get deeper insight into your authentic self.

3. Taking responsibility for expressing your real self.

   No one is going to come up to you and say: *"Now you can be your authentic self."* So don't wait for an invitation and/or permission from someone else. Instead, be proactive in recognizing and expressing your true nature.

4. Holding yourself to a higher standard of authenticity.

   Each and every day, express even more of your authentic self, and before you know it, it'll become a habit.

5. Expressing your magnificence.

   All of us have special talents and gifts. A big part of being authentic is to express these gifts and talents to their fullest extent.

6. Not being afraid.

   Fear sometimes stops us from being ourselves. So rather than indulging fear, ask yourself: *"What would it mean if I be, do, and live, being true to my authentic nature?"* Tackle any obstacles to expressing your true self courageously and quickly.

   Now it's true that, at times, being authentic may result in undesirable results, such as pain in the form of disapproval from the people you love. But realize that this is a very small price to pay for being true to *yourself.*

   Finally, remember that what others think of you is none of your business anyway.

7. Truly celebrating your progress.

   As you notice yourself operating from your true nature even more consistently, feel proud of yourself and reward yourself for making progress.

8. Improving in the areas that need to be addressed.

   All of us have areas that we can improve in. Identify and prioritize the areas that make the most sense for you to address. Then devise and execute an action plan to address these.

9. Cutting yourself some slack when you slip up.

   Being authentic is challenging, especially when so many people are not. When you do slip up and/or fail to live to your own expectations, don't be too hard on yourself. Be kind and forgiving with yourself.

In closing, I suggest that you consider the words of Norma T. Hollis, author of the book, *Ten Steps to Authenticity*:

> *"Once you find your authenticity, you must decide to live it.*
> *How? By being aware that the things you say and do on*
> *a daily basis support the inner voice that is speaking*
> *to you, which is the foundation of your authentic core."*

W O R D S *of* W I S D O M

"The single biggest problem in communication
is the *illusion* that it has taken place."

G EORGE B ERNARD S HAW
(1856–1950)
British (Irish-Born) Dramatist, Literary Critic,
and Leading Figure in 20th Century Theatre

CHAPTER 42

Master the Most Important Skill in Life

COMMUNICATION WITH SELF AND OTHERS

We spend most of our lives communicating, and yet the subject of communication is not given enough focus in our homes, schools, universities, and even in our workplace. Most of what we pick up about communicating is really through trial and error. The net result is that most of us are not good communicators.

But what exactly is "communication"? Most people think of it in relation to dealing with others, e.g., conversations, making presentations, doing speeches, providing instructions, listening to others, and so on.

The fact is that communication actually exists on **two levels**:

1. Communication we have with our self
2. Communication we have with others

Communication with our self takes place in the form of:

- The **thoughts** that we have
- The **meaning** we give to our thoughts
- What we **say to ourselves** on a regular basis
- The **manner** in which we talk to ourselves

Communication with others takes place in the form of:

- The extent to which we **listen** to others
- The **meaning** we give to what others say
- What we **say** to others
- The **manner** in which we talk to others

At this stage, you may be thinking: *Is there a relationship between the two forms of communication? Which one is most important to master?*

Here's what I think. To sustain an outstanding quality of life, it's important to master communication—both with yourself and with others. However, if you had to pick one to accelerate the mastery of, I would recommend mastering the communication you have with yourself. This is because the quality of our communication with ourselves drives, to a large extent, the quality of communication we have with others. As Lao Tzu, the eminent Chinese philosopher, once said: *"Knowing others is wisdom, knowing yourself is enlightenment."*

Communication with self is a huge subject, and almost everything in this book has been designed to address this at a deep level—from examining to questioning to reimagining. As such, I won't go into any further discussion on this topic here, but instead will focus on strategies to improve your communication with others.

HOW TO IMPROVE YOUR COMMUNICATION WITH OTHERS

A key point first—mastering communication is a lifelong journey, and not a quick fix. Recognize that no matter how good you already are, there is an even higher level of excellence. Therefore, commit to mastering the science and art of communication. Having clarified that, there are three broad strategies to focus on. Even though each one can improve the quality of your interaction, you will get *exponential* benefits when you apply these strategies in an **integrated manner**.

The three strategies are:

1. **Become aware of your communication styles.** As mentioned at several other places in this book, awareness is the first step to any change. The more aware you are of how you communicate with others, the more you can catch yourself when you indulge in communication styles that don't serve you.

   To become aware of how you communicate with others, answer the following questions:

   - *How do others perceive your communication style?*
   - *What types of people do you have problems communicating with?*
   - *What emotions do you normally feel when communicating with others?*
   - *What is your listening-to-talking ratio?*
   - *To what extent are you comfortable with silence?*
   - *To what degree do you confuse telling with communicating?*

2. **Plan your communication.** It's critical to plan your communication, because when you fail to plan—you plan to fail. To help you plan your communication, I recommend that you use the *"Results-Driven Communications Framework,"* as illustrated in the diagram on the next page. By using this framework, you'll bring more awareness and clarity to your communications. And when you communicate with awareness and clarity, you achieve your communication outcomes effectively and efficiently.

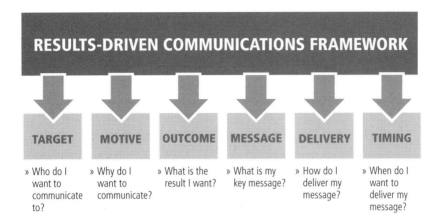

RESULTS-DRIVEN COMMUNICATIONS FRAMEWORK

TARGET	MOTIVE	OUTCOME	MESSAGE	DELIVERY	TIMING
» Who do I want to communicate to?	» Why do I want to communicate?	» What is the result I want?	» What is my key message?	» How do I deliver my message?	» When do I want to deliver my message?

3. **Seek first to understand before being understood.** In Stephen R. Covey's best-seller, *The 7 Habits of Highly Effective People*, Habit 5 is this: ***"Seek first to understand, then to be understood."*** The more you do this habit, the more effective you'll be at communicating. Henry Ford, founder of Ford Motor Company, put it best when he said: *"If there is any great secret of success in life, it lies in the ability to put yourself in the other person's place and to see things from his point of view—as well as your own."*

To master this habit, here's what I recommend:

- **Be fully present.** Be nowhere else, or in other words, "be now here." To be fully present in your conversations is the *absolute foundation* to mastering communication.

- **Be comfortable with silence.** Use the power of silence. If you have nothing to say, say nothing. As American success coach and author Jack Canfield so elegantly put it: *"Listen a hundred times. Ponder a thousand times. Speak once."*

- **Be a better listener.** There is a reason why we have two ears and only one mouth. As Larry King, America's famous talk show host, said: *"I remind myself every morning: nothing I say this day will teach me anything. So if I'm going to learn, I must do it by listening."*

- **Be a detective.** Master the science and art of asking high quality questions, of both yourself and others.

- **Go beyond the words to understand the meaning.** A common problem in communication arises from the difference in meaning we each give to the same words. If you find yourself reaching an impasse in your communication with others, make sure you're able to look beyond the words and understand the underlying meaning. You may be surprised to find that even though you may be using different words, the underlying intent and meaning may be exactly the same, or vice-versa. In one of his speeches, South African civil rights leader Nelson Mandela said: *"If you talk to a man in a language that he understands, that goes to his head. If you talk to him in his language, that goes to his heart."*

- **Read body language.** Research indicates that over 50% of our communication is non-verbal—our body language reveals a lot more than words can. So to really understand what's going on in your interactions with others, learn to become sensitive to interpreting people's body language. The key is to hear what isn't being said verbally.

Finally, there's one time in particular when it's essential to keep communicating, that's when you're at odds with another person. Though you may need time for reflection about the conflict, don't create a distance that goes on too long. Continue to talk to each other and work through your differences, integrating the communication skills discussed in this chapter.

WORDS *of* WISDOM

"Gratitude is not only the greatest of virtues,
but the parent of all others."

CICERO
(106–43 B.C.)
Roman Statesman and Philosopher

CHAPTER 43

Develop Your Strongest Muscle

WHAT'S YOUR STRONGEST MUSCLE?

Before we begin, grab a pen and some paper, and for the next 10 minutes, write down everything that you're grateful for in your life. Be as specific as possible. OK—ready, set, go!

How many items do you have on your list? If you have fewer than 50, please continue writing until you have at least that many. If you're stuck, let me offer a few suggestions. Think about everything that you're grateful for—no matter how big or small.

Focus on:

- All the people who love you—both family and friends
- People who have supported you to get to where you are
- Your talents
- Your health
- What you've accomplished in your life
- The lucky breaks you've had
- Where you live and the lifestyle you enjoy
- The resources you have
- Experiences and magic moments you've had the privilege of being a part of

Now have a look at your list. And as you review it, notice how you feel. Are you feeling happy? Are you feeling successful? Are you feeling lucky? Are you feeling fulfilled? Or at the very least, are you feeling better than before you started doing this exercise? Am I right about that?

The change in how you're feeling is not surprising. It's because gratitude has the power to overcome almost any disempowering emotion. When you feel gratitude, fear disappears, doubt disappears, and your problems disappear, even if temporarily. The feeling of gratitude lifts your energy and your mood. Think of gratitude as a muscle—a muscle so strong that it's capable of lifting you out of negative emotion and into a positive state of mind.

HOW TO BUILD STRONGER GRATITUDE MUSCLES

Even though gratitude is such a powerful emotion, most people don't feel it often enough. This is because experiencing gratitude is *a conscious choice*. And that conscious choice is **to direct your focus to what's already great in your life and how blessed you actually are *right now*.**

So how do you feel more gratitude, more often? The key is to: *Be grateful, Do gratitude, and Live with gratefulness.* Here are some ideas to get you started:

1. **Be grateful.**
   - Notice, appreciate, and feel all the good that currently exists in your life. Ask yourself:
     › *What can I be grateful for?*
     › *What's already great in my life?*
   - Manage your desires. When the constant search for more is moderated, the natural balance of gratitude is restored.

2. **Do gratitude.**
   - Help others—when you shift the focus off yourself and on to assisting others, you instantly feel a sense of gratitude. Being of service to others is a gift you give yourself.

- Express your gratitude. Sir Isaac Newton, the great English physicist, was quoted as saying: *"If I have seen further, it is by standing on the shoulders of giants."* As you read this quote, ask yourself: *"Who have been the giants in my life?"* Make a list of everyone who's been instrumental in helping you throughout your life. Find a way to express your gratitude to these people—whether that be face-to-face, making a phone call, or writing a letter.
- Schedule a ritual—a specific day and/or time where you consciously focus on experiencing gratitude.
- Buy a gratitude journal and write in it every day—make this a daily habit.

3. **Live with gratefulness—live as if:**
   - Every day is a gift.
   - You are guided.
   - You are here for a special purpose.
   - Everything in your life has been purposely orchestrated to serve you.

What else can you add to the above list of ideas?

WORDS *of* WISDOM

"Man is made by his belief.
As he believes, so he is."

Bhagavad Gita
The sacred Hindu Scriptures

CHAPTER 44

Eliminate
Limiting Beliefs

YOUR BELIEFS SHAPE YOUR LIFE

A belief is something that you accept as true about something or someone, including yourself. For example, how would you answer if I asked you, *"Are you intelligent?"* Simply put, if you accept it as true that you are intelligent, you'll answer "yes." If you don't accept it as true that you are intelligent, you'll answer "no." It's immaterial what the *absolute* truth is because, for you, **whatever you choose to believe is the absolute truth**!

At the simplistic level, for example, you have a choice to believe or disbelieve anything or everything presented in this book. The result of that choice will determine the extent that you implement the suggestions you find here, and it will therefore determine the value you get from your investment in my book.

Your beliefs are very important because they influence how you think, who you become, what you do, and how you live your life. Specifically, the beliefs you hold about life, yourself, work, relationships, money, spirituality, and people directly influence your quality of life. In conclusion, **one could argue that the sum total of all your beliefs equals the sum total of the quality of your life**!

Here's an interesting irony — even though our lives are shaped by the beliefs we hold, in most cases, we don't consciously choose our beliefs. Our beliefs are formed over time, as a result of our conditioning, our experiences, and our observation of other people's experiences.

We also do not consciously evaluate the consequences of the beliefs we hold. According to Don Miguel Ruiz, author of the best-seller, *The Four Agreements,* 95% of the beliefs we have stored in our minds are nothing but lies, and we suffer because we believe all these lies.

The good news, however, is that beliefs can be changed and *do* change over time.

DO YOU WANT TO CHANGE ANY BELIEFS?

Before you can identify the specific beliefs which are limiting you, you first need to become conscious of your beliefs in general. To determine the beliefs you hold, let's do an exercise. But before we start, let me share some tips in order to maximize the value of this work:

- First, have a pen and paper handy.
- Write as fast as you can so as to prevent your rational mind from over-analyzing, justifying or, worse still, denying.
- Don't hold anything back because only once you're aware can you choose to do something different.

OK, let's start, and complete these two steps:

1. Make a list of all of your key beliefs.
   Specifically ask yourself what you accept as true about:
   - Life
   - Relationships
   - People
   - Yourself
   - Money
   - Spirituality
   - Health
   - Career/business
   - Success

2. Review each of the beliefs you identified above, and ask yourself:
   a. *Does this belief help me or limit me?*
   b. *Do I want to or need to eliminate this belief?*

Be brutally honest as you answer the above questions.

HOW TO CHANGE A BELIEF

Once you've identified the beliefs you want to change, go through the following three-step process for each limiting belief that you want to eliminate.

1. **Create an urgency for change.**
   Changing beliefs is easiest when there is a strong desire to change. And most of us only change when we experience enough pain with the status quo. To feel the pain, you need to consciously become aware of the cost of hanging on to the limiting belief. Cost can obviously be in many forms: missed opportunities, failure to be who you want to be, failure to do what you want to do, and so on. To create urgency for change, ask yourself the following questions:

   • *What has this belief cost me to date? What have I failed to be or do because of this belief?*
   • *What is it costing me now to hold on to this belief?*
   • *What will be the cost if I hang on to this belief for the next 5, 10, 15, or 20 years?*

2. **Identify a more empowering replacement belief.**

Ask yourself:

- *What is a more empowering belief that should replace my current limiting belief?* For example, if your limiting belief was: *"I am too old to start my own business,"* a replacement belief could be: *"It's never too late to do anything, as long as I'm committed."*
- *How would my life be better with this new empowering belief?*

3. **"Condition" the new belief.**

Research indicates that it takes 21 days to form a habit. So for the next 21 days, live with your new, more empowering belief. Celebrate and reward yourself as you condition the new belief. Be kind with yourself if you slip back into your old patterns.

As I discussed in the chapter, the beliefs you hold affect the quality of your life. And perhaps the most crucial type of belief is what you believe to be true about yourself. What beliefs in this area are holding you back the most? Once you've identified at least two such beliefs, use the three-step process above to empower yourself with more supportive replacement beliefs. For a more in-depth coverage about belief systems, I highly recommend Anthony Robbins' book, *Awaken the Giant Within.*

WORDS *of* WISDOM

"The most important single influence
in the life of a person is another person
. . . who is worthy of emulation."

PAUL D. SHAFER
(1902–1984)
President, Packer Collegiate Institute

CHAPTER 45

Build Your Winning Team

WHAT'S A CRITICAL FACTOR FOR SUCCESS?

What enables families, communities, businesses, and even countries to be highly successful?

Of the many factors, including vision, leadership, and persistent action, a critical common factor behind all successful enterprises is a **winning team.** As clichéd as it sounds, *Life is a team sport.* And to win in the sport of life, you must assemble a winning team.

WHAT'S A "WINNING TEAM"?

Your "winning team" is composed of people who can, and are willing to, provide you with the appropriate mentoring and/or coaching to help you create and sustain your dream life. The people in your winning team should meet the majority—if not all—of the following criteria:

1. They possess wisdom and experience which you respect.
2. They are already at a point that you want to reach. This could be because:
   - They are already similar to the person you want to become.
   - They've done what you want to do.
   - They live in a way that you'd like to live.

3. They have your best interests at heart.

4. They're willing to share their expertise and experience with you.

HOW TO ASSEMBLE YOUR WINNING TEAM

There are two types of teams to assemble:

- Your **Board of Directors**—a small core group whose wisdom and guidance you value across all areas of life.
- Your **Specialist Advisors**—people with skills, knowledge, and experience in specific areas of life.

To build each of your above teams, go through the following three steps:

1. **Identify the people you want on your team.** You'll have some choices to make. How wide do you cast your search? Do you only go for the people you know, or do you cast the search much wider? The answer depends, in part, on your desire and ability to get access to the people that you want on your team. For example, given the choices, it would be great to have Warren Buffet as a financial mentor. However, you need to balance that with the odds of getting access to him.

2. **Be clear on the support you want.** Clarity is power. Be very clear on the support you're looking for. Also, be very specific on what that might mean from the mentor's perspective. The more clear you are, the more impressive you'll come across when approaching the people you'd like to mentor and/or coach you.

3. **Approach the people on your list.** Prior to making contact, be clear about your plan for approaching the people you've chosen. How will you make contact? What will you say? How will you follow up? How will you convince them to help you? Having a plan is obviously not enough. You need to make contact. In case you start to have second thoughts, remember that the worst that can happen

is that they can say "no," in which case you're not any worse off anyway. However, if they do say "yes," the upside is huge.

The following diagram can be used to capture details about your team:

HOW TO LEVERAGE YOUR WINNING TEAM

To get the most out of your team, I recommend the following:

1. Develop a relationship with your team. Look to add value to your team first. What is it that you can do to add value to their lives? Seek and act on opportunities to be of service to your team members.

Never take them for granted.

2. Whenever faced with situations where another perspective may be useful, ask yourself:
   - *Given the same situation, what would my Board of Directors and/ or my Specialist Advisors do?*
   - *Why?*

3. Seek counsel from your team on issues and/or opportunities where their guidance would be of immense value to you.

It's important to follow up the advice and ideas you receive from your team with an appreciative phone call, note, or email about how things turned out. Appreciation will place you in a state of gratitude and will also help reinforce these relationships.

WORDS *of* WISDOM

"Each man has his own vocation; his
talent is his call. There is one direction
in which all space is open to him."

RALPH WALDO EMERSON
(1803–1882)
American Author, Poet, and Philosopher

CHAPTER 46

Spend 80%+ Time in Your Personal Greatness Zone

WHAT DO WE ALL HAVE IN COMMON?

What do an American president, an English executive, a Chinese doctor, an Irish psychologist, a Swedish hair stylist, and an African school teacher have in common?

The number of hours in a day. It doesn't matter who you are, what you do, or where you're from—the one constant is that we all have just 24 hours available each day. Often people complain about not having enough time, but guess what? You can't have more time because that's not an option. Actually, the more important question is: ***What do you do with the time you have?***

Whether or not you realize it, we all consciously choose where and how we spend our time. And our choices have a dramatic impact on the quality of life we experience. This is because how we spend our time drives what we do or fail to do, which in turn determines the results we get and how we feel. Over time, one could argue that our cumulative decisions about how we spend our time determine our destiny.

YOUR PERSONAL GREATNESS ZONE

All of us have what I term as our very own **Personal Greatness Zone**, or PGZ for short. As illustrated on the next page, your PGZ comprises activities that you love doing and that you are great at. Coaching, for example, is one of the activities in my PGZ. It's something that I'm passionate about and also very skilled at. So it's not surprising that when I'm coaching, I feel like I'm on a roll. I experience tremendous joy. I am completely present. I feel totally fulfilled.

I would go as far as to say that, whenever you're in your PGZ, you emanate the very best part of you. You shine your light brightly.

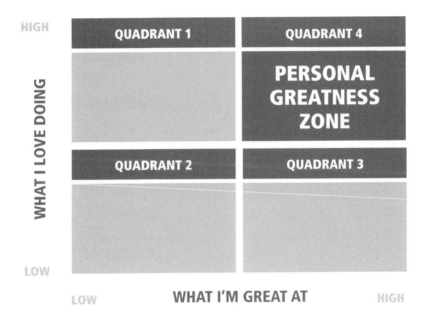

SPENDING TIME IN YOUR PERSONAL GREATNESS ZONE

To maximize your personal and professional fulfillment, you should aim to spend at least 80% of your waking time in your **Personal Greatness Zone (PGZ).**

However, most people don't spend enough time in their PGZ. Why?

It's mainly because most people:

1. Don't clearly know what activities are in their PGZ.

2. Are fearful and/or don't believe that they can make a comfortable living doing activities in their PGZ.

3. Spend more time than is necessary on activities that they don't enjoy and that they're not very good at either (i.e., activities in Quadrant 2).

What about you? What proportion of your waking time is spent in your PGZ? What, if anything, is preventing you from spending more time in your PGZ?

No matter what your reasons are, be aware that there are practical consequences to not doing what you love. In their book *Success Built to Last,* authors Jerry Porras, Stewart Emery, and Mark Thompson articulate the dangers: *"The harsh truth is that if you don't love what you're doing, you'll lose to someone who does! For every person who is half-hearted about their work or relationships, there is someone who loves what they're half-hearted about. This person will work harder and longer. They will outrun you. Although it might feel safer to hang on to an old role, you'll find your energy is depleted and, miraculously, you'll be the first in line for the layoffs when they come."*

To increase the time you spend in your PGZ, I recommend the following approach:

1. **Believe in yourself.** Believe that you can make an abundant living doing what you enjoy doing and what you're good at. Belief is essential because if you don't believe it's even possible, then you won't even take the first steps. In the words of Malcolm Forbes, publisher of *Forbes* magazine, *"Success follows when you do what you want to do. There is no other way to be successful. The biggest mistake people make in life is not trying to make a living at doing what they most enjoy."*

2. **Identify activities in your PGZ.** Think about the activities that you really enjoy. The ones you enjoy so much that time disappears and you're totally present in the moment. You feel energized. You feel fulfilled and on purpose. Of the activities that you do enjoy, which ones are you good at? You feel exceptionally strong when doing these. What are some activities that others think you do really well?

3. **Develop a plan.** Once you know the activities in your PGZ, you need to develop a plan that will allow you to spend more time there. In developing your plan, ask yourself:

   - *Who can help me in my transition?*
   - *How can I create more demand for activities in my PGZ?*
   - *How can I get paid well for activities in my PGZ?*

   To create more time for activities in your PGZ, review the diagram on the next page for recommendations on what to do with activities that aren't.

	QUADRANT 1	QUADRANT 4
WHAT I LOVE DOING (HIGH)	Find ways to get better at these so that eventually they become Quadrant 4 activities.	**PERSONAL GREATNESS ZONE**
	QUADRANT 2	QUADRANT 3
(LOW)	Stop doing them yourself— eliminate these if possible or outsource them to someone for whom these would be Quadrant 4 activities.	Either change your perception so that these become Quadrant 4 activities or spend only the minimum necessary time.

LOW **WHAT I'M GREAT AT** HIGH

4. **Execute your plan.** Words are cheap and action is everything. Do something every day that will allow you to move forward. Monitor your progress and reward yourself for advances.

Don't settle for a good life when you can have a great one! Celebrate your strengths by spending 80% of your time, or more, in your Personal Greatness Zone.

WORDS *of* WISDOM

"The most powerful form of leverage in
the world, your mind, has the power to
make you rich or make you poor."

ROBERT KIYOSAKI
Author, *Rich Dad, Poor Dad*

CHAPTER 47

Attract Financial Abundance

A HOLISTIC FRAMEWORK

Money is a resource—one that can be used for making a difference in your life, in the lives of others, and for society as a whole. There are numerous books that cover how to make money—I don't intend to add to that list. Instead, what I offer on the next page is a holistic framework—one that outlines the different components that come into play in attracting financial abundance into your life.

I recommend that you use the Framework to:

1. Assess your current situation regarding money, including identifying any beliefs and/or strategies that might be holding you back, and

2. Generate ideas to attract more financial abundance into your life.

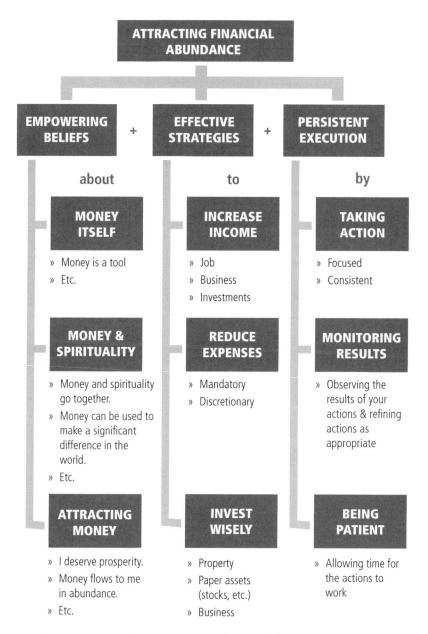

After working with the Framework, which beliefs and strategies are your highest priorities to change? Which ideas for attracting abundance do you want to start working with first? What else can you think of that would be helpful as you begin?

WORDS *of* WISDOM

"Many people die with their music still
in them. Why is this so? Too often it is
because they are always getting ready to
live. Before they know it, time runs out."

OLIVER WENDELL HOLMES, SR.
(1809–1894)
American Poet and Writer

CHAPTER 48

Live As If It's Your Last Day

WE ALL HAVE AN EXPIRATION DATE

In one of the books I read, it said something along the lines of: *"I wish I could grasp the reality that I am going to die one day, so I can finally start to really live."* Whether we like it or not, we all have an expiration date. And to paraphrase American statesman Benjamin Franklin, the only certainty other than taxes is physical death.

With so much "busyness" taking up our time and energy, the fundamental question to keep at the forefront of our minds is: *"How can I live each day to its fullest extent?"*

And as clichéd as it sounds, *Life is not measured by the number of breaths you take, but the moments that take your breath away.*

WHAT IF TODAY WAS YOUR LAST DAY?

Imagine if a God or some higher power came to you and said: *"Today could be your last day on earth. Whether or not you live another day or several decades will depend on how fully and joyously you live today."* As you ponder this scenario, let me ask you:

- *How would you live the day?*
- *Who would you to choose to spend the day with?*

- *What would you do?*
- *Where would you go?*
- *Who would you call? What would you say?*
- *What thoughts would you think?*
- *Would you worry about the same things that you typically worry about?*
- *Would you do some of the things that you've always wanted to do but never had the time and/or courage to do?*

Leaving aside the specific answers to the above questions, most people would, I suspect, live the day somewhat differently than a *normal* day. Most people would experience more joy, love, happiness, and gratitude on this day than they experience on their *normal* days.

HOW TO LIVE MORE FULLY

Rather than waiting for a summons from a higher power, **my suggestion is that you plan, schedule, and live at least one day a month as if it *were* your last day on earth**.

Live this day as if it were the ultimate gift. Don't hold *anything* back. Be *even more*. Do *even more*. Live *even more*. And when you finally go off to bed, perhaps exhausted, and as your head hits the pillow, you can feel proud of yourself for having lived the day to the max.

I guarantee that exercising this ritual will not only energize and rejuvenate you, but it will also expand your consciousness. It will enable you to achieve and sustain a more integrated and holistic life.

WORDS *of* WISDOM

"Self-love is not opposed to love of other
people. You cannot really love yourself
and do yourself a favor without doing
other people a favor, and vice versa."

DR. KARL MENNINGER
(1893–1990)
Dean of American Psychiatry

CHAPTER 49

Love Yourself
No Matter What

HOW MUCH DO YOU LOVE YOURSELF?

You might think this is a bit strange, but bear with me. Please answer the following question: *"On a scale of 1 to 10 (1 = not at all, 10 = completely), how much do you love yourself?"*

If your answer was a 10, then I congratulate and applaud you. If your answer was anything other than a 10, then please read on.

My next question is: *"Why are you not at level 10 on self-love?"* Ponder this for a few minutes before reading further.

Though I don't know your specific answer to the second question, I will take a wild guess. My guess is that your reasons would fall into one or more of the following categories:

- There is some part of yourself that you're not happy with (e.g., your finances, your relationships, or your health).
- You feel that there is something missing in your life (e.g., a loving partner, your ideal job, more money).
- You sometimes, or often, have thoughts that you believe are bad or inappropriate, and you can't seem to shake them off for good.
- You've done things in the past that you're not proud of.
- You sometimes, or often, behave in a manner that is inconsistent with how you normally see yourself.

In summary, you have a certain benchmark about "What a level 10 on self-love looks like" and you don't believe that you measure up to that benchmark. And you also believe that until you achieve that benchmark, you're not worthy of completely loving yourself. Well, how close was I to guessing your reasons?

WHY IS LEVEL 10 IMPORTANT?

Regardless of your specific reasons for not being a level 10 on self-love, you may be thinking: *"Why does it matter if I'm not a level 10 on self-love?"* Let's explore the reasons.

When you're more loving to yourself, you're more loving to others, and also more forgiving. When you love yourself more, you feel happier and more at peace. When you're more loving to yourself, your relationships tend to be stronger as well. This is because you view relationships as a place you go to give, rather than to take. When you love yourself completely, you behave more authentically, because you're not driven by the need to please others. More importantly, though, by completely accepting and loving yourself, you reveal your true divine nature and by doing that, you also inspire others to do the same.

So, all in all, loving yourself completely is not only great for you, it's also great for others, and for all of humankind.

HOW TO LOVE YOURSELF EVEN MORE

To strengthen your level of self-love, I recommend the following four strategies:

1. **Relax your rules for self-love.** Earlier, you diagnosed what was preventing you from being at a level 10 on self-love. To move closer to a level 10, you have two choices. Either to:
   - Take the necessary actions to resolve whatever is holding you back, and/or

- To change your rules about what has to happen for you to love yourself more.

For example, if what's holding you back is some mistake you made in the past, realize that whatever you've done in the past cannot be undone, and no extent of beating yourself will change a thing. The only sensible and wise solution is to learn the lessons, let go, and move on.

2. **Be more loving to yourself.** What do you *say* to others to let them know that you love them? To what extent do you say the same things to yourself?

For example, do you say, *"I love you"* to the people you love? Assuming that you do, when was the last time you looked in the mirror and said, *"I love you"* to yourself? I know it sounds weird and many of you at this stage are probably doing the *"I don't think so"* head movement. However, trust me on this, and give it a go. You have nothing to lose, since no one is watching anyway! While it may initially feel awkward, like most things it will get more and more enjoyable as you do it regularly.

3. **Do more self-love.** What do you do to show your love to other people? To what extent do you do the same things for yourself? As you answer this, you'll discover strategies that are specific to you. This will enable you to develop your menu of self-love strategies.

As an example, my menu of self-love strategies includes:
- Having a massage
- Taking time out for myself
- Reading inspirational books
- Watching movies that make me laugh and inspire me
- Learning new skills
- Creating something of value
- Buying myself a present
- Going for a swim

- Being of service to others (e.g., coaching, teaching, giving inspirational talks)
- Being playful
- Really listening empathically

4. **Live with more self-love.** Put self-love high on your priority list. Realize that self-love is not a selfish act, but a highly unselfish act. Since you can't give to others what you don't have, you can't be loving to others unless you feel love for yourself.

In closing, I leave you with the following quote from Thomas Merton, a 20th century author and Trappist monk:

"What can we gain by sailing to the moon if we are not able to cross the abyss that separates us from ourselves?"

Words *of* Wisdom

"There is more hunger for love and
appreciation in this world than for bread."

MOTHER TERESA
(1910–1997)
Humanitarian and Advocate for the Poor

CHAPTER 50

Develop Your Menu
of Appreciation

WHY IS APPRECIATION CRITICAL?

A basic human need is to feel appreciated—that is, the need to be acknowledged, to be recognized, and to feel special. This need applies across all contexts—work, family, and community. Just to be clear, this is not a desire that some have and others don't. Instead, it is a basic psychological need shared by all human beings.

When we feel appreciated, we feel good. When we feel good, we treat ourselves better. We treat others better as well.

WHY DON'T WE FEEL ENOUGH APPRECIATION?

If I asked you the question, *"Do you feel appreciated as much as you would like?"* how would you answer? Most of us, I suspect, could do with more appreciation and acknowledgment than we currently experience.

So as far as appreciation is concerned, what causes the gap between what we desire and what we actually experience? There are three key reasons:

1. **Lack of clarity.** We are unclear about what needs to happen for us to feel appreciated. In other words, we are unclear about our own rules for appreciation.

2. **Reliance on others.** We rely solely on others to appreciate us and don't appreciate ourselves enough.

3. **Not sharing our rules.** Even if we know our rules for appreciation, we don't often share these rules with the people who are important to us. Therefore, even when others *do* appreciate us, we may not feel appreciated if their rules for appreciation are different from our own.

HOW TO FEEL MORE APPRECIATED

In order to feel more appreciated, take the following three steps:

1. Establish your **Menu of Appreciation (MOA)**. Your MOA, as illustrated in the diagram below, is a two-by-two matrix that captures all the things that, if said or done, would make you feel appreciated.

	LITTLE THINGS	**BIG THINGS**
OTHERS	**QUADRANT 1** What are some little things that others can say or do which will enable me to feel even more appreciated?	**QUADRANT 4** What are some big things that others can say or do which will enable me to feel even more appreciated?
SELF	**QUADRANT 2** What are some little things that I can say or do to appreciate myself?	**QUADRANT 3** What are some big things that I can say or do to appreciate myself?

To develop your MOA, ask yourself the following two questions:

- *What are some little things and big things that I can say or do to appreciate myself?*
- *What are some little things and big things that* others *can say or do that would make me feel appreciated?*

Record your answers in the Menu of Appreciation that you created.

2. The items in Quadrants 2 and 3 of your MOA are within your control—so schedule and act on these.

3. Share items in Quadrants 1 and 4 of your MOA with people who are important in your life. The more that other people are aware of your rules for appreciation, the more likely they will appreciate you in a manner that will resonate with you.

It's also important to remember that the people around us will "mirror" our behavior. In other words, appreciation is contagious! So make it a habit to express appreciation to others more often.

WORDS *of* WISDOM

"We are what we repeatedly do.
Excellence, then, is not an act, but a habit."

ARISTOTLE
(384–322 B.C.)
Greek Philosopher

CHAPTER 51

Develop
Powerful Rituals

WHY HAVE RITUALS?

According to the *Oxford English Dictionary,* a ritual is *"a series of actions or types of behavior regularly and invariably followed by someone."*

If you apply the above definition, you'll conclude that you already have rituals in many areas of your life. The most obvious daily rituals we all have are those of showering, brushing our teeth, going to work, and sleeping. These are activities that we do at specific times of the day without question.

Rituals increase consistency, because you don't evaluate, every time, the value of the associated actions. Establishing rituals, therefore, is a great strategy—especially for action(s) you know are good for you, but that you aren't regularly doing yet. Typically, these actions are important but not necessarily urgent.

HOW TO FORM RITUALS

There are five steps involved in establishing rituals:

1. Identify some new specific rituals by asking yourself the following two questions:

- *In what areas of my life do I need and want more discipline?* (e.g., health)
- *What actions do I know I need to take more consistently?* (e.g., exercising regularly)
2. Commit to following through.
3. Schedule a regular date and time for the above action(s).
4. Take action(s) and reward yourself for following through.
5. Maintain consistency.

EXAMPLES OF RITUALS

Below are examples of other useful rituals across the different areas of life:

- *Business*—weekly status meetings, annual strategic planning days, quarterly performance reviews, team development days
- *Family*—family day, date with your kids, date with your spouse, celebrating birthdays
- *Finances*—annual planning day, monthly budgeting day, weekly tracking of budget versus actual, half-year net position review, yearly financial position review
- *Growth*—yearly goal planning, quarterly progress review, regular reading time
- *Contribution*—day to spend with less privileged, organizing an annual charity event
- *Health*—annual health review, quarterly checkup, weekly exercising routine
- *Mental*—daily meditation, weekly journal writing

After reading this chapter, which new rituals do you want to establish?

W O R D S *of* W I S D O M

"There is evidence that human beings possess
a range of capacities and potentials—multiple
intelligences—that both individually and in
consort can be put to many productive uses."

H O W A R D G A R D N E R
Author, *Multiple Intelligences*

CHAPTER 52

Grow Your
Holistic Intelligence

WHAT IS INTELLIGENCE?

Most people have a very limited view of "intelligence." When people think of intelligence, they typically think of IQ—the traditional view of intelligence. Even the *Oxford English Dictionary* subscribes to a very narrow definition of it: *"the ability to acquire and apply knowledge and skills."*

I define intelligence as: *"your ability to tap into all the available resources, either consciously or subconsciously, within yourself and/or others in order to achieve a specific worthy outcome in the most effective, efficient, and harmonious manner."*

MULTIPLE LEVELS OF INTELLIGENCE

In my view, human beings possess many types of intelligence—nine in all. The different types, as depicted and described on the next page, are like different pieces of our **holistic intelligence** jigsaw.

HOLISTIC INTELLIGENCE

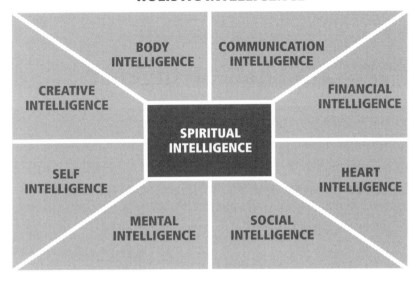

1. **Spiritual intelligence.** This is your ultimate intelligence—your inner compass, your guidance system, your faith in the universal power.

2. **Body intelligence.** This intelligence keeps you alive and functioning day in and day out—without you having to think about it. It's the intelligence that keeps your heart beating, even when you're asleep.

3. **Creative intelligence.** This is your skill to create something out of nothing, to think outside the box, to generate innovative ideas, to be original.

4. **Self intelligence.** This is your knowledge of yourself—why you do what you do, your personality, your beliefs, your emotions, your sense of identity, and so on.

5. **Mental intelligence.** This is the traditional view of intelligence, typically related to IQ. It's the intelligence that relates to your verbal and numerical skills and your ability to make subtle distinctions.

6. **Social intelligence.** This is your capacity to relate to others in an effective manner.

7. **Heart intelligence.** This is the extent to which you are tuned in to the *signals* you receive from your heart—the feeling about whether something is good or bad, or right for you or not.

8. **Financial intelligence.** This is your ability to understand and apply the laws that lead to financial abundance.

9. **Communication intelligence.** This is your ability to communicate with yourself and others in an honest and constructive manner.

HOW TO NURTURE YOUR HOLISTIC INTELLIGENCE

Listed below is a three-step process to enhance your holistic intelligence.

1. **Acknowledge.** Accept that you possess many levels of intelligence. Our holistic intelligence is probably our most untapped natural resource.

2. **Plan.** A fundamental law of nature is *"You lose what you don't use,"* and this principle applies to your various intelligences as it does to everything else. In order to nurture your intelligences, you need to exercise them. So begin now, by preparing a plan to enhance all your intelligences.

3. **Leverage.** When you need to evaluate options and make decisions, ensure that you tap into all the relevant intelligences to generate the optimal outcome.

While intelligence is valuable, it's important to consider the wider context as well—in other words, how your intelligence is applied *in the world.* As American essayist and poet Ralph Waldo Emerson famously remarked, *"Character is more important than intellect."*

WORDS *of* WISDOM

"Man is a goal seeking animal.
His life only has meaning if he is reaching
out and striving for his goals."

ARISTOTLE
(384–322 B.C.)
Greek Philosopher

CHAPTER 53

Apply the Accelerated Goal Achievement Formula

THE IMPORTANCE OF GOALS

It is often said that goals are dreams with a deadline. For lasting success and fulfillment, we need to continually set goals and strive to achieve them. Goals provide an excellent vehicle for ongoing personal growth and also enable us to:

- **Be**come all that we are capable of
- **Do** more
- **Live** more fully

So it pays to master the science and art of achieving goals. On the following pages, I outline an **"Accelerated Goal Achievement Formula (AGAF),"** which can be used to:

1. Set meaningful goals.
2. Ensure that in setting and achieving goals, you consider all the necessary dimensions.
3. Diagnose the areas that you need to focus on in order to fast-track the achievement of your goals.

ACCELERATED GOAL ACHIEVEMENT FORMULA

The Accelerated Goal Achievement Formula has eight parts.

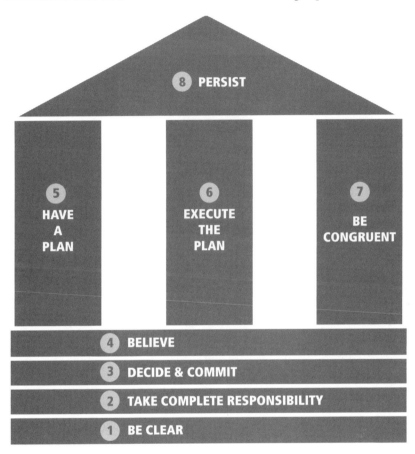

1. **Be clear.**
   - *What is your goal?* (Outcome)
   - *Why is it a must for you to achieve this goal?* (Reasons)
   - *What is your target date for achieving your goal?* (Date)
   - *How will you know if you've achieved your goal?*
     (Evidence procedure)

- *What is your starting position in relation to the goal?* (Current position)

2. **Take complete responsibility for:**
   - The goal
   - The process for achieving the goal

3. **Decide and commit.**
   - *What are you prepared to do to achieve the goal?*
   - *What are you NOT prepared to do to achieve the goal?*

4. **Believe that:**
   - You deserve to achieve your goal.
   - You will find a way to achieve your goal.
   - Appropriate people, resources, and situations will show up to help you achieve your goal.

5. **Have a plan.**
   - *What are the key activities?*
   - *What is the required order and sequence of these activities?*
   - *What is the time frame? What are the interim milestones?*
   - *What resources do you need?*
   - *Who has achieved what you want? What could you learn from their experience?*
   - *Who else could help you get to your goal faster?*

6. **Execute the plan.**
   - Take action.
   - Observe the results you get from the actions you take.
   - Be flexible and refine your plan as necessary.

7. **Be congruent.**
   - Align your thoughts, words, and actions with what will help you make progress toward your goal.

8. **Persist.**
   - Recognize the inherent delay between taking action and seeing results.
   - Be patient. Remember the saying, *"Infinite patience produces immediate results."*
   - Don't give up.
   - Continue to review, refine, and evolve your plans.

As I discussed earlier in the book, remember to enjoy the journey as you work toward your goals. And keep in mind that the key is *who you become* on the journey of striving toward those goals.

WORDS *of* WISDOM

"Anything worth remembering
is worth writing down."

ANONYMOUS

CHAPTER 54

Four Journals You Must Own

A PROFOUND PRACTICE—JOURNALING

The act of writing has enormous power. Writing generates greater clarity. It creates a permanent record of positive memories. And if you choose to believe it, by putting things on paper, you even engage the universal intelligence as a co-creator of your dream life. As such, I recommend that you buy and use at least the following four journals:

JOURNAL	WHAT TO CAPTURE?	WHY?
GRATITUDE JOURNAL	» Everything that you are grateful for. This includes people in your life, your life experiences, who you are, what you have, your memories, and so on.	» Fulfillment in life is a function of the gratitude you feel—the more grateful you are, the more fulfilled your life is. » The more conscious you are of ALL that you are grateful for, the more gratitude you feel.
DREAM JOURNAL	» All that you want to be » All that you want to do » All that you want to have » How you want to live	» The act of writing your dreams triggers the universal intelligence to conspire with you to turn your dreams into reality.
IDEAS JOURNAL	» Ideas » Opportunities » Possibilities » What-ifs?	» Sometimes the ideas we come up with are great, but the timing to implement the ideas may not be ideal. » Keeping a record of our ideas enables us to revisit these ideas at a later date, when the timing may be right.
MAGIC MOMENTS JOURNAL	» Special moments in your life » Moments that made you laugh or smile or even shed a tear of joy or gratitude	» "Life is not measured by number of breaths you take, but the moments that take your breath away."

To jump-start your efforts, I offer the following advice from Sheppard B. Kominars, PhD, a writing instructor and author of a book on journaling called *Write for Life*. He suggests that instead of worrying about the time you'll need to give to journaling, you should focus on the energy you'll get back from the practice. "Consider your efforts as energizing instead of time-consuming," he says. Kominars adds that you can even write down what you'll do with the additional energy.

WORDS *of* WISDOM

"Words form the thread on which
we string our experiences."

ALDOUS HUXLEY
(1894–1963)
Author, *Brave New World*

CHAPTER 55

Connect with the 99% World

OUR TWO WORLDS

There are two parallel worlds we all live in—the world of **form** or **matter,** and the world of the **formless** or **spirit**.

The world of form or matter is the world that we perceive through our five senses. We have a language to describe what we see, hear, or feel. This is also a world of duality—right versus wrong, good versus bad, peace versus war, and so on. Most people think that this world is the real world. In Hindu philosophy, however, the material world is referred to as *Maya,* which literally means an illusion.

On the other hand, the world of the formless or the world of spirit is a bit of a mystery to most of us. The spiritual world is hard, if not impossible, to perceive through our normal senses. For example, has anyone really seen the spirit or the soul? What does it look like? If there is a God, what does God look like? It is not easy, if not actually impossible, to answer such questions.

Of the two worlds, which one do you believe is more powerful?

As I see it, the spiritual world is the 99% world and the material world is the 1% world. In other words, I believe that the spiritual world is infinitely more powerful than the material world.

BARRIERS TO EXPERIENCING THE SPIRITUAL WORLD

Other than the lack of belief, one of the main barriers to experiencing the spiritual world is the inadequacy of our language. When we use our conventional language to describe the spiritual experiences (including the experiences of synchronicity, intention, faith, intuition), the most we end up doing is creating mental constructs, or labels, of these experiences. It's like the difference between "knowing" something and "experiencing" something, e.g., knowing the word "water" versus feeling joy while swimming in the ocean on a hot summer day.

HOW TO EXPERIENCE THE SPIRITUAL WORLD

Listed below are some basic practices for getting more in tune with the spiritual world.

QUIET YOUR MIND	» Unless you reduce your mental chatter, it is very hard to connect to the spiritual world. It is often quoted that "Silence is the language of god."
SUSPEND YOUR DISBELIEFS	» Rather than looking for a scientific explanation and proof for everything, learn to trust in the knowingness of everything. Even though you can't see electricity, you do know that it exists.
TRUST IN INTUITION	» For example, when you get an unexpected phone call from someone you were just thinking about, don't dismiss the incident as a coincidence. Instead, trust that this was an intuitive connection between two spiritual beings.
RESIST LABELING	» Avoid the temptation to put labels to your experiences. Instead, just relish the experience.
SPEND TIME IN NATURE	» Water, trees, plants—these are all beautiful examples of the spiritual power in action. By spending more time in nature, you can feel the vastness of the spiritual world.
BECOME A PRACTITIONER	» Do practices that help you to go deep within, e.g. meditation, yoga, prayer, silent contemplation.

After reading about these practices, which ones do you think will be most important to you in your spiritual journey? Can you think of any other specific practices that would help you connect to the 99% World?

WORDS *of* WISDOM

"Too many people overvalue what they
are not and undervalue what they are."

MALCOLM FORBES
(1919-1990)
Publisher of *Forbes* magazine

CHAPTER 56

Tattoo Eight Words on Your Forearm

POWERFUL WORDS

While you may not actually want a new tattoo, placing the following words in a prominent place where you'll see them often can have a powerful, positive self-reinforcing effect:

I
AM
BETTER
THAN
I
THINK
I
AM.